The why and how of this book

The Dr Ann website (**www.teenagehealthfreak.org** and **www.doctorann.org**) has now received over 40,000 emails from young people about their health. There have also been quizzes on the website to find out what young people know about health matters such as drugs, sex and other things that worry them. Emailed concerns about the use of drugs – both legal and illegal – make up the main content of this book: Are all drugs bad for you? Why do teenagers take drugs? Do you get hooked on drugs straightaway? How can you tell if someone is taking drugs? What happens when you smoke weed? How does ecstasy affect your body? If you are caught in possession of drugs, will you be sent to jail? What is the current legal situation over cannabis? These and hundreds of other questions are answered by the experts, using carefully researched materials, and relying on many years of clinical experience.

The book is mainly for young people aged around 13 and over, though many adults will certainly learn a thing or two. Research shows that the more knowledge young people have about drugs at an early age – before they actually try drugs – then the more likely they are to delay experimenting with them, and if they do try drugs, they are more likely to try them in safer ways.

Really reliable information, put over in an even-handed, non-moralistic way, is the key to this book. So whether you are aged 13 or 40, try reading it and learn all about this vital area of life. It is all around us, but rarely spoken about openly, so information you can really trust is hard to come by.

The Dr Ann website was originally set up because of the success of the books *Diary of a Teenage Health Freak* and *The Diary of the Other Health Freak*, both published in new editions by Oxford University Press in 2002. If you go onto the **www.teenagehealthfreak.org website,** you can catch up with Pete Payne and all his worries – about his spots, his love life, his feelings about drugs, his parents, his parties – all in his daily diary. Or you can read the books – and anyone, like Pete Payne, can also find out what worries and probably the world, and how to get this book.

AIDAN MACFARLANE is a consultant paediatrician and public health doctor who ran the child and adolescent health services for Oxfordshire. He is now a freelance international consultant in teenage health.

ANN McPHERSON is a general practitioner with extensive experience of young people and their problems. She is also a lecturer in the Department of Primary Health Care at the University of Oxford.

As well as *The Diary of a Teenage Health Freak* and its sequel *The Diary of the Other Health Freak*, their other books include *Mum I Feel Funny* (which won the Times Education Supplement Information Book Award), *Me and My Mates*, *The Virgin Now Boarding*, and *Fresher Pressure*. They also published a book for parents about the teenage years called *Teenagers: the agony, the ecstasy, the answers*. Their most recent books have been *R U a Teenage Health Freak?* and *Teenage Health Freak: Sex*, a companion to this book. The authors also run the extremely successful website on which this book is based – **www.teenagehealthfreak.org** – which receives around 250,000 hits a week and recently won the BUPA communication award.

Authors' acknowledgements

We would like to thank: all the teenagers who emailed us with questions, and all their parents for having them (the teenagers) in the first place; Liz and all the other team at Baigent for their work on the website; Mike and Jane O'Regan for all their support and their funding; Ben Dupré for all his wonderful patience and 'suspect' sense of humour when helping us with the editing. We would also like to thank all the sources of information which we have used, including: all the websites that have made the job so much easier; Magnus, Tamara and Gus Macfarlane for their contributions; Colin Blakemore and Susan Greenfield for their wise observations on the subject; the 'Study Safely' booklet which has been an excellent source; and all those other young people who helped us and hadn't done their brains in with drugs.

Note

The answers we have given to the questions in this book are based on our personal clinical experiences as doctors when dealing with similar clinical problems. Young people reading the book will, we think, be helped by the answers that we have given. However, it is impossible for us to offer advice in such a way as to deal with all aspects of every individual's health problem. Therefore if you, as a reader of this book, have any continuing doubts or concerns about your health problem, we would strongly advise you to consult your own medical practitioner.

To preserve the true flavour of the originals, we have not changed or edited the language or spelling of the emailed questions used in this book. However, in the few cases where real names are used, these have been changed to protect the anonymity of the senders.

the truth

drugs

OXFORD
UNIVERSITY PRESS

Great Clarendon Street, Oxford OX2 6DP

Oxford University Press is a department of the University of Oxford.
It furthers the University's objective of excellence in research, scholarship,
and education by publishing worldwide in

Oxford   New York

Auckland Bangkok Buenos Aires Cape Town Chennai
Dar es Salaam Delhi Hong Kong Istanbul Karachi Kolkata
Kuala Lumpur Madrid Melbourne Mexico City Mumbai Nairobi
São Paulo Shanghai Taipei Tokyo Toronto

Oxford is a registered trade mark of Oxford University Press
in the UK and in certain other countries

British Library Cataloguing in Publication Data available

ISBN 0-19-911170-7

1 3 5 7 9 10 8 6 4 2

Printed in Great Britain
by Cox & Wyman Ltd., Reading, Berkshire

Contents

THE LOW-DOWN ON DRUG HIGHS   7

1 DRUGS – THE LEGAL, ILLEGAL, GOOD AND BAD   8
What exactly is a drug?

2 HOW MANY, HOW OFTEN, HOW BAD?   13
Who does drugs and what do they take?

3 EXPERIMENTING WITH LIFE, LOVE AND CHEMICALS   19
Why do drugs?

4 FITTING IN OR FALLING OUT?   24
Bullying and pressures to take drugs

5 IT'S NOT JUST YOU – IT'S THOSE AROUND YOU, TOO   30
Does doing drugs affect others in your life?

6 CAFFEINE – THE WORLD'S MOST POPULAR DRUG?   36
Tea, coffee, cocoa and colas – are they really drugs?

QUIZ 1 HOW DRUGWISE ARE YOU?   40

7 MONEY UP IN SMOKE   41
Smoking

8 UNDER THE INFLUENCE…AND OUT OF CONTROL   49
Alcohol and what it does to you and your brain

9 CANNABIS – PLEASE AT LEAST KNOW THIS MUCH   58
The highs, the lows, the in-betweens

10 USING THE WEED: THE MYTHS AND THE PROBLEMS   65
The uncertainties about using cannabis

11 DON'T DO IT BUT IF YOU DO, USE KNOWLEDGE   72
Cannabis: the definite bad effects

QUIZ 2 TRUTHS AND LIES ABOUT ALCOHOL,   78
       SMOKING AND CANNABIS

12 INHALING, SNIFFING AND POPPING   79
Solvents and poppers: what they are and what they do

13 THE SPEED TRAP – WHEN EVERYTHING IS OVER THE LIMIT 85
Amphetamines and speed

14 DESIGNER DANCE AND CHANCE DRUG   89
Ecstatic about ecstasy?

15 TRIPPING WAY BEYOND REALITY   95
Hallucinating on acid and magic mushrooms

16 THINKING OF CHECKING IN YOUR LIFE?   101
Heroin, cocaine and crack

17 A SPORTING CHANCE OF LOSING EVERYTHING   108
All about sports drugs

18 GETTING TESTED, GETTING BUSTED   113
Illegal drugs, testing and the law

19 DAMAGE LIMITATION – KNOWING THE FACTS   118
*Precautions if you are going to do drugs,
and where to get help*

QUIZ 3 THE REAL NASTIES…   123

NEED TO FIND OUT MORE?   124

INDEX   127

The low-down on drug highs

Taking chemical substances – whether inhaling them, drinking them, eating them or injecting them – can be almost an obsession, both for those who do drugs and for those who don't. Cries of delight on one side, and cries of horror on the other.

But it isn't all black and white. You need to look at the evidence and reach your own conclusions. Some drugs *are* worse than others – and it doesn't help to pretend that they are all the same. Another problem is that we still do not know what damage some drugs will do to our brains in the long term.

The main thing is to be informed, to know as much as you can about what is bad and what is not so bad, to understand the huge range of possibilities: from the legal to the illegal; from the soft to the hard; from the caffeine in your cola to the crack up your nose; from the inhaled to the hallucinogen; from fun to the funeral; from pushing to prison.

It is all here – with chapters covering what a drug is, why people take drugs, the pressures concerned, the effect on others, the individual drugs, the laws and what happens when you break those laws. Also – most essentially – what drugs do to your body and brain, and how to help yourself and get help when you need it.

Finally, it is worth remembering that just because an illegal drug is used a great deal, this does not necessarily mean that it is either a good idea, or safe.

1 Drugs

the legal, illegal
good and
bad

WHAT EXACTLY IS A DRUG?

When the word 'drug' is mentioned, most people think 'illegal drugs'. But actually, the word 'drug' means far more than that. It is important to know about all the different kinds of drugs – natural, medical and illegal – and to know their good and their bad effects, and how they affect different people in different ways.

● THE GOOD, THE BAD, THE DANGEROUS

Doc – **hi how r ya! How many drugs are good????**
13 year old girl.

Dear 'How many drugs are good' – Drugs include a whole range of different chemical substances that affect our bodies in different ways. The majority of the thousands of drugs that have been developed over the last 50 or 60 years have some good effects. But, like illegal drugs, almost all of these 'legal' drugs can have bad effects as well. Some people are allergic to specific 'drugs' such as penicillin, which cause them to come out in red itchy spots on the skin. Some drugs have even nastier unwanted effects. You can also take too much of any drug and get very ill. Furthermore, some people are particularly sensitive to even quite common 'drugs' like aspirin, which can make holes in the wall of their stomach and cause them to bleed a lot. The general rule with any drug is not to take it unless you really need it, just in case it causes any problems.

Dear Ann — **are all drugs bad or are some drugs good for you?** 13 year old boy.

Dear 'Person interested in different types of drugs' — The word 'drug' is used to cover different chemical substances that have different effects on our bodies and minds. At one end, there are 'drugs' like caffeine, which is found 'naturally' in tea and coffee. Then there are artificially created medicinal drugs, such as aspirin and paracetamol, which help us feel better when we have headaches or colds. You can buy these 'over the counter' at different types of shops (chemists, newsagents, supermarkets, etc), and they are safe for most people as long as they are taken in the recommended dose on the box. There are also more complicated medical drugs, like antibiotics, heart medicines, medicines to stop epileptic attacks, etc. Because these drugs tend to have more side effects, they have to be prescribed by doctors. Then there are the illegal drugs — if you use these, then you may get into trouble with the police, as well as damage your health.

Doc — **what are the worstest drugs if I do take 'em?** 16 year old boy.

Dear 'Worst drugs wonderer' — Heroin and crack cocaine are considered to be the illegal drugs that cause the greatest harm. The latest surveys indicate that about one in a hundred of 11- to 15-year-olds had used heroin or methadone in the last year, and 4% had used stimulants like cocaine and crack, as well as ecstasy, amphetamines and poppers.

Dear Doc — **do our bodies produce any drugs naturally?** 14 year old boy.

Dear 'Natural drug producer' — The definition of a drug is a chemical substance that 'comes from outside our body' and that we 'inhale, take by mouth or by injection, or sometimes some other way'. But... our bodies do produce chemicals that are very like some of the drugs which people take. For instance, when you exercise very hard, your body produces chemical substances called 'endorphins'. These 'natural' body chemicals are very similar in their chemistry and their effects to a group of drugs sometimes taken illegally, called 'morphines'. So get exercising and you may get a 'high'.

● **WHY THE LAW ON DRUGS?**

Dear Dr Ann — **why are some drugs against the law if you take them?** 14 year old girl.

Dear 'Curious about the law' — Some drugs are illegal because they change the way our brain sees the outside world, and although they may make us (at least for some of the time) feel better, happier, more relaxed, they may also make us behave in strange and unpredictable ways that can frighten ourselves and other people. Another problem is that many illegal drugs are very 'addictive', meaning that once you start taking them, you have a craving for taking more and more. Finally, most illegal drugs (as well as many legal ones!) actually have other effects which may harm both our bodies and our minds. There are some drugs that are prescribed medically – like heroin, which can be used to stop people feeling pain – but may also get used illegally without a doctor's prescription because it can also make people feel very good.

Dear Doctor Ann – **what is the proper use for barbiturates, can they be against the law and what happens if you overuse them?** 16 year old boy.

Dear 'Interested in barbiturates' – Barbiturates used to be prescribed by doctors to treat epilepsy and to help people who had trouble sleeping. However, more effective drugs with fewer side effects have been developed to treat these medical problems. Some people used barbiturates illegally because it made them feel relaxed and sociable. Barbiturates are especially dangerous because the difference between a normal prescription dose and an overdose, which can cause someone to stop breathing, are very close. The other problem is that people do become dependent on them and find it difficult to stop taking them.

Hi Doctor Ann — **I've been worried about my older sister lately, she's been acting very strange.** So i decided to read her emails to see if i could find out what was going on. The emails i read are very worrying, **she's taking some sort of drug i believe but i have never heard of it. It's called valium.** Can u tell me what it actually is & effects of it. She won't like it if she finds out that I've been reading her emails, but I'm really worried about her!

Dear 'Worried about sister taking valium' — Valium is a drug that is sometimes prescribed by doctors to help calm people down. Before you start worrying about whether your sister is taking something really bad, it would be best to try and find out whether she is on it because it has been prescribed by her doctor, or whether she is taking it illegally. But you will have to tread carefully. You have found yourself in an awkward situation because you know something that you have found out by 'snooping', even if you did it for the best of reasons! Valium belongs to a group of drugs called benzodiazepines, which are sometimes prescribed by doctors to help people with anxiety, but it is also very addictive. This can mean that if you take valium regularly, you end up wanting more and more valium, and when you try to stop it, you feel awful. Don't keep this information about your sister to yourself; share it with a grown-up you trust – probably your mum or dad. They may be able to put you straight. Your sister may be cross with you in the short term about you reading her emails, but she will probably understand why it makes you anxious.

2 How many,
How often,
how bad?

The use of drugs by young people, whether medical drugs, tobacco, alcohol or illegal drugs, has increased over recent years. Although there are definite dangers to using any drugs, most young people only use illegal drugs occasionally, and usually as an experiment to see what they are like. Most young people experimenting with drugs – whether illegal or legal – don't come to the attention of the law, even if there is increasing evidence that they may be damaging their brain. But it is absolutely essential, whether or not you experiment with drugs, to know about them and to know what their different effects are.

● **HOW MANY TAKE THEM?**

Dear Doctor Ann – **how many people take drugs?** 15 year old girl.

13

Dear 'Curious about numbers of people taking drugs' – As far as the drug tobacco is concerned, about a third of young people under the age of 16 smoke regularly, a third have tried and given up, and a third have never tried. The number of 15-year-olds who have ever taken an illegal drug (mainly cannabis) is around one in five, but at a younger age it is much less. The figures for young people over the age of 15 show that of young people aged 16 to 19, about half have tried drugs at some time in their life (again mainly cannabis), a third had used a drug in the last year, and about one in five had used a drug in the last month.

Dear Doctor Ann – **how many people take illegal drugs at 14.** 14 year old boy.

Dear 'Curious about 14-year-old drug users' – The most recent information is that around one in ten young people aged 14 are trying illegal drugs. Cannabis remains by far the most commonly used drug and is used more by boys at this age than by girls. Cannabis use also increases with age: 2% of 11-year-olds have used the drug, compared with 28% of 15-year-olds, with the sharpest increase being for 14- to 15-year-olds.

Doc – **is there a greater number of young people taking drugs than before and what do they take?** 14 year boy.

Dear 'Inquirer about increase in drug-taking' – Yes there is. In a survey done in 1998, around 7% of young people aged 11 to 15 had used an illegal drug in the last month and this had gone up to around 9% in 2000. Among 15-year-olds, 14% had tried a drug in 2000, compared with 11% in 1998. By far the most popular drug was cannabis. Other rates were 4% (cocaine, ecstasy, amphetamines), and heroin, 1%.

Eighty per cent of 15-year-olds have NOT tried drugs – so you are part of the 'in' crowd if you do NOT do drugs.

Dear Dr Ann – **do English kids do more drugs than in other countries like in Europe?** I need to know for a project at school. 14 year old girl.

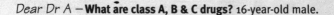

Dear 'Wondering about European drug taking' – A European survey of schoolchildren showed that teenagers in Britain are more likely to have taken illegal drugs and to drink alcohol than teenagers living anywhere else in Europe. They are also near the top of the league when it comes to smoking cigarettes.

● DIFFERENT TYPES, DANGERS AND EFFECTS

Dear Dr A – **What are class A, B & C drugs?** 16-year-old male.

Dear 'Drug classifier' – In the UK, illegal drugs are classified into three main classes according to how 'bad' the illegal drug is considered to be. How likely you are to get put in jail, how long you will be put in jail, and how big a fine you pay will depend on the class of drug involved. Class A drugs are heroin, methadone, cocaine, crack, ecstasy and LSD. Class B drugs include amphetamines (speed), taken by mouth, and barbiturates. Class C drugs are the lowest class and include 'mild' amphetamines (such as slimming drugs), anabolic steroids, and valium if obtained illegally. Sometime in 2003, cannabis will be moved from being a class B drug to being a class C drug.

Dear Dr Ann — **What is the most dangerous drug?** 12 year old girl.

Dear 'What is the most dangerous drug' — This is a difficult question to answer because it depends on what you mean by 'most dangerous'. There are many different dangers from drugs — for instance any drug, even aspirin, can be dangerous if you take too much of it! Some drugs cause addiction, some drugs can kill, and some give all sorts of nasty side effects. Probably the most dangerous 'illegal' drug at the moment is 'crack' because it is so, so addictive that once you have started taking it, it is very, very difficult to stop and you can't think of anything else but getting more of it. But

if you look at the drug that kills the most people, then there is no question that tobacco smoked over a long time is the most dangerous drug, and it is also very addictive.

Dear Dr Ann — **do drugs have different effects on different people?** 14 year old girl.

Dear 'Effects enquirer' – Drugs definitely do affect people differently. This applies as much to 'medical drugs' as it does to 'illegal drugs'. The more research that is done, the more doctors find that medical drugs can affect children very differently from adults – and may even have totally opposite effects. The same drug can also affect different children, different young people and different adults in different ways. This is why if one medicine/drug doesn't work, then it is a very good idea to try another one to see if that works. For instance, if you have acne and one cream doesn't work, then it is always worth trying another. If aspirin doesn't cure a headache, then maybe paracetamol will. And not only do different drugs affect people in different ways, but also the amount of the same drug needed to have an effect in treating one person may be very different from the amount needed to treat another person. This is also true of all illegal drugs. One person smoking cannabis may get very sick and throw up, whilst another person may find that it has very little effect of any kind. Sometimes a drug will have an effect on all people who take it – for instance, anyone trying 'crack' is likely to get addicted!

Dear Ann – **do you know what other teenagers think about us taking drugs?** 16 year old girl.

Dear 'Wanting to know teenagers' view on drug-taking' – I am assuming that you mean illegal drugs here, because the view of teenagers on taking *legal* drugs in order to get well if you are ill would probably be all good. However,

NO ENTRY

young people are surprisingly tough on people who use *illegal* drugs, especially if they do it at school. When 12- to 19-year-olds were asked what they thought should happen if someone was discovered to be using illegal drugs in school on a regular basis, over half said they should be expelled from school, one in three said they should be dealt with within the school situation, and just over one in ten said they should be suspended from school for some time. All schools have a policy of 'zero tolerance' to drug-taking in the school. What schools do if someone is caught taking drugs will therefore depend on whether it occurs in or out of school, what the drug is, and whether they are selling drugs to other pupils. Expelling a teenager from school because they had used an illegal drug at some time in their lives might mean that about half of all schoolchildren would be expelled (if someone knew about their drug use).

3 Experimenting with life, love and chemicals

WHY DO DRUGS?

Around half of young people try illegal drugs – but why? It appears to be part of experimenting with life in general. To learn how to cope with the huge menu of experiences life has to offer, we need to 'taste' them to see what they have got going for them. In general, there is an expectation by teachers, parents and politicians that young people will do what they are told when it comes to things that adults consider good and bad but, but, but... as adolescents, we think differently and we seem to have to learn for ourselves by experimenting. It is one quite natural and effective way of learning.

● **WHY, OH WHY?**

Doc – **why do teenagers take drugs?** 13 year old boy.

Dear 'Wondering why' – There are a number of different reasons given by young people aged 16

19

when they are asked why they take drugs. There is, of course, the fact that they are easily available. Then there are the main reasons given by young people themselves: around half say they did it out of curiosity, in order to see what they are like, just for fun, etc. A third say they did it because their friends were doing drugs and they felt left out and pressurized into it. And finally, around one in five said that taking drugs was a better alternative to worrying about something else in their lives, or that it made them less anxious. Interestingly, although over three out of four young people agree 'that drugs harm your health', three out of four also agree that most young people will try out drugs at some time.

Dr Ann — **why do people get tempted to smoke cigarettes or do drugs?** 15 year old girl.

Dear 'Why do people get tempted to smoke and do drugs' — There are lots of reasons why people get tempted by cigarettes and drugs. The commonest reason is simple curiosity — because they want to know what it is like. Fortunately, after one or two tries they decide not to try it again, especially with cigarettes, as it is rarely very enjoyable the first time. But reasons that make people keep on taking drugs and smoking cigarettes include feelings that if you don't do them, you won't be one of the crowd and won't look big. Unfortunately, then they get addicted and can't do without them. This sort of pressure is now considered to be a form of bullying by many people. But where drugs are concerned especially, the bullies are really the pushers who make a lot of money by getting people hooked on drugs.

Dear Doctor Ann – **why do people want to smoke cigarettes?** 14 year old boy.

Dear 'Wanting to know why people smoke' – There is a whole variety of reasons why people should want to try new things – nothing simple I am afraid. Up to about the age of 14, many young people feel very strongly that it is wrong to smoke – because of its effects both on the smoker's health and the health of others around who have to breathe in the smoke passively. Many young children who have parents who smoke will keep trying to make them give up. Then, quite suddenly, around the age of 14 to 15, young people want to experiment with new things in life – one of these is to try out smoking, and another is to take illegal drugs. The trouble with cigarettes is that they are easily available and are also very, very addictive. You probably only need to smoke three or four cigarettes, and then it begins to get more and more difficult to give up.

Doctor – **I'm on drugs and i can't help it cuz im depressed and I haven't told anyone.** 16 year old girl.

Dear 'Depressed' – The problem about being depressed and trying many of the illegal drugs (cannabis for one) is that if you are depressed before taking the drug, it will probably make the feeling even stronger and the drug will make you more depressed, not less! The best way of dealing with depression is to talk to someone about how you feel – a friend, your parents, your doctor. If the talking by itself doesn't work, then there are some *medical* drugs that will help you feel less depressed, and it is worth going to see your doctor and talking to him/her about the way that you feel. You don't *have to* explain that you have been trying illegal drugs, though it might help your doctor to help you if they knew about it.

● **DO YOU STAY ON DRUGS FOR EVER?**

Doctor Ann — **if you take drugs once do you get hooked on them straight away?** 15 year old male.

Dear 'Worried about getting hooked straight away' — With some drugs like tobacco, you can be hooked after as few as four or five cigarettes, but I suspect that we are talking about the more illegal drugs here? Illegal drugs like cannabis are not thought to be addictive – but some people find that if they are taking it regularly, they become psychologically dependent on it. Another problem is that most people smoke cannabis with tobacco and get addicted to the tobacco as a result. Other drugs, like crack, cocaine and heroin, are extremely addictive and very, very difficult to get off. So it all depends on the type of 'drug'.

The reason why most young people experiment with drugs in the first place is a mixture of curiosity, availability and being surrounded by other people who are doing them. The reasons for misusing drugs are more complex and involve other factors like having low self-esteem, living in poverty, living in a family where other people are also doing drugs. But still, somewhere around half of all young people don't even experiment with drugs.

Doc — **once you're on a drug do you go on for ever?** 14 year old boy.

Dear 'Eternal worrier' — Of all young people who have experimented with illegal drugs (say around half of all 15- to 16-year-olds), around 19 out of 20 will just experiment with them and then stop, and one in twenty will actually abuse a drug and get into problems. These tend to be young people who feel bad about themselves in other ways, or who have mental health problems. The number of young people taking drugs goes down rapidly after the age of around 20 to 25 because they have to start earning serious money doing serious jobs.

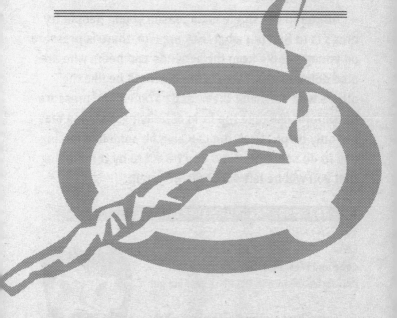

Fitting in
or falling out?

4

Although the single main reason young people try drugs is to find out what they are like, there is pressure on young people from their friends and peers who are also doing drugs. There is the desire to be like the others who surround them, and at times, the pressure to conform can take the form of bullying. Bullying may not only be physical, but can also be someone forcing you to do something you don't want to by threatening that you will be left out of an 'in' group.

● **PRESSURE, PRESSURE EVERYWHERE**

Dear Ann — **many of my friends smoke dope and i feel that they are trying to pressurize me into it. HELP?** 14 year old girl.

Dear 'Pressurized' — I wonder what you mean by 'pressurize'? If you are

surrounded by friends, all of whom are smoking cannabis, and they are saying 'Why don't you try it too?', ask yourself 'Why should I try it too?'. You don't necessarily have to give way to the pressure from your friends. Before you decide what to do, you need to learn all the facts that you can about the bad and not so bad effects of illegal drugs – by reading through this book. Don't let your friends make up your mind for you.

Dear Ann – **my mate is taking drugs and he wants me to get started on them! What should I do??** 14 year old boy.

> *Dear 'Boy with mate taking drugs'* – The best thing is not to give in – you don't have to do drugs at all. If you do do drugs, it's best to learn as much as you can about them first. You have a number of places that you can choose to find out more about drugs: you can read about drugs in the rest of this book, you can look them up on the web, you can get information from lots of organizations that are there to help (see pages 124 to 126), you can talk to your friends about them – but I suspect they may know less about them than you think.

Dear Doctor Ann – **why do people pressure me into taking drugs?** girl age 13.

> *Dear 'Pressured into taking drugs'* – If it's your friends who are pressuring you, then it's probably because it makes them feel good, as they may feel insecure about taking drugs themselves. If it's the drug pushers who are pressuring you, then it's because they want you to get hooked on drugs so

they can make money out of selling them to you. DON'T be pressurized, stick with what you want to do and what you think is right. If they're real friends, they'll still like you and be friends. If not, then they are not worth having as friends!

Dear Doctor Ann — **what should I do if someone forces me to have drugs?** 13 year old boy.

Dear 'Not wanting to be forced into drugs' — You will be glad to hear that people do not go around actually 'forcing' drugs on other people, although they may put a lot of pressure on them. People take drugs because they want to see what they are like, because they find it a 'social' thing to do with other people who also take drugs, or because they find it a better alternative to their real lives. If someone offers you an illegal drug, it is OK to say no and you will still be in the crowd.

Doc — **at least half of my class at school either smoke or take drugs and 3 quarters of them have tried it.** I have not and i am feeling left out and a bit of a wimp – what should i do? 14 year old boy.

Dear 'Haven't tried drugs' — You are NOT a wimp – in fact exactly the opposite, because it sounds to me as if you clearly have a mind of your own, that you are strong-willed and you are making sure that you get your own way when you want to. What you should do is to find out as much as you can about smoking cigarettes and illegal drugs (by reading the rest of this book and getting information from other sources – see pages 124 to 126). It may feel like half your class are taking drugs, but the facts actually show otherwise and that far fewer than half will have tried them. Good luck and stay independent of other people's opinions – stick with your own.

Resisting pressure by others can be very difficult. Find a friend who feels the same way as you do. Being one can make you an easy target, but being two makes the target twice as difficult to hit on.

● ARE THESE FRIENDS?

Dear Doctor Ann – **every time i go out with my friends i always drink** they say i make them laugh and persuade me to drink and stuff but im not sure if i have a problem… ! **i am depressed but i dont drink cuz of that !! Do i need help?!** 17 year old girl

> *Dear 'Depressed drinker' –* **It sounds as though some of these friends might not be such good friends after all. Being persuaded to drink to keep them amused may not be good for you, and they may be laughing at you rather than with you. Beware that you are not making a fool of yourself. Talk to one friend whom you really trust about what they think, and next time these 'friends' push drink on you, resist and see if they are still friends. And yes, you do need some help if you are depressed, and you may be drinking to cover it up.**

Dear Doctor Ann — **I have tried smoking and hated it but every time my mate asks me if i want one i have to say yes because i don't want to sound chicken. How can i tell him i don't like it?**

Dear 'Not wanting to appear chicken' — Saying NO and/or telling your mate you don't like or want to smoke is not being chicken. In fact, your mate is being a bully by pushing you to smoke and making you feel bad if you say no. Why not try suggesting your mate doesn't smoke and suggest he is a weakling to be smoking because he can't stop. Also, suggest all the things that the money saved from not smoking could be spent on.

Dear Doctor Ann — **my best friend **** offered me some drugs. Is he a friend?** 14 year old boy.

Dear 'Person who shouldn't have a best friend like this' — A friend who tries to persuade you to do something illegal, like trying illegal drugs, is probably just showing off, or they are trying to get you to join in so that he can feel less alone in what he is doing. If he is a real friend, he will still be your best friend even if you say 'no thanks' — try it and see.

Dear Doctor Ann — **my friend thinks another friend put something in her drink and she can't remember what happened to her. Can someone give you a drug without you knowing?** 17 year old girl.

Dear 'Girl with friend given a drug without her knowing' — There is a drug 'Rohypnol' which people have used to 'spike' other people's drinks. The effect of the drug is to make you rapidly unconscious and also to make you forget anything that happened. Possessing Rohypnol without a doctor's prescription is an offence under the Misuse of Drugs Act, with a maximum sentence of two years and an unlimited fine. It can be very difficult to tell when a drink has been 'spiked', but if someone is ever in the slightest worried that their drink has been tampered with, then obviously they shouldn't drink it.

Hi Dr Ann – **I have just moved towns and the other night i was given a joint and i smoked it!! and now they are trying to get me to try other drugs they say they will make me feel really good.** Smoking the joint was alright but someone told me it is dangerous and i am frighten to try the other drugs please help – don't know what to do. Are joints that bad for you?? 15 year old boy.

Dear 'Just moved towns' – When you are with a new group of people and you want to be 'in' with them and are trying to make friends, it is very natural to go along with what everyone else is doing in order to be accepted by the group. But you will also be respected by your new friends if you show them that you have a mind of your own and won't necessarily go along with what they suggest. Smoking cannabis is common amongst young people, and like any drug, can have problems (see page 69 for the side effects of cannabis), but on the whole, it actually has fewer problems than most of the other illegal drugs around. However, there are many other drugs that are dangerous because they are highly addictive – like heroin and cocaine. So watch out for these and don't forget how addictive tobacco can be, even on its own.

5 It's not just you –
it's those
around
you, too

Different illegal drugs affect people in a wide range of different ways. However, these drugs can affect not only those who are taking the drugs, but also those intimately involved with the drug taker, whether it is their unborn child, other members of their family, or their friends.

● **AFFECTING RELATIONSHIPS**

Dr Ann – **how can you tell if someone is taking drugs? Please answer soon.** 15 year old girl.

Dear 'Wanting to know signs of drug-taking' – People will often not be openly aware that someone else they know is taking drugs. But there will often be little changes in that person's behaviour – like them being more

secretive, moody, or seeming more 'distant' – which change their relationships with those around them. Furthermore, they may smell of alcohol, cigarettes or cannabis. The most likely way to find out directly if someone is doing drugs is if they choose to talk to you about it. Another common way is finding their drugs or the 'equipment' they may use for taking certain kinds of drugs. In the case of cannabis, the drug itself may be either in the form of 'grass', which looks like dark green cut-up leaves, or 'hash', which may be green or brown hard lumps of cannabis resin. Other drugs come in different forms – ecstasy as tablets, and Lysergic acid as drops of dried liquid on small squares of blotting paper. The effects of drug-taking on people's behaviour depends on what the drug is. If someone is smoking cannabis regularly, they may appear to be rather 'vague' or 'not with it', which is why cannabis is also known as 'dope'.

Dear Doctor Ann – **my male friend smokes, drinks and takes drugs. The smoking and drinking doesn't bother me but the drugs do.** I've tried confronting him but he just shuts me out. 15 year old girl.

Dear 'Friend to a drug-taker' –
Drug-taking can come between friends who care about one another – and this can be a real problem. It must present a very real dilemma for you because you obviously care a great deal about your friend, but unfortunately you can't *make* him stop. Let him know that you are still a friend, but don't be afraid to say what you think about him using drugs, though this may not change him.

Dr Ann — **what do i do if I find a drug in my friend's pocket after a party?** I'm very, very worried because I really mind about her – she is a good friend. 14 year old girl.

Dear 'Finder of a drug in a friend's pocket' — This is difficult. The most important thing is that you stay her friend. If you are so worried about her, why not talk to her about it and see what she says. You don't actually say which drug you found in your friend's pocket, but whether you feel that you want to take it further depends on you. Whether it is cannabis or more dangerous drugs, you shouldn't feel that you have to keep things that you feel uncomfortable about secret. You may want to tell your mum or someone else that you trust.

Even if most drug-taking in young people is experimental and short-lived, it does take money and time, it can distract you from work, and it can distract you away from being social with certain groups of friends – and you may find yourself rubbing shoulders with some pretty dodgy characters. Getting arrested for possessing or dealing with drugs will have a profound effect on your family, as well as on yourself. This will also apply if you die from drug misuse!

● DIRECT EFFECTS ON OTHERS – BABIES

'Scuse me Doctor Ann — **but how do drugs like heroin affect babies?** 14 year old boy.

Dear 'Worried about heroin and babies' — I assume you mean unborn babies developing inside their mothers?

There is a wide range of drugs, both legal and illegal, that can affect the unborn baby. In general, it is best not to take any drugs at all during early pregnancy unless you have to. The following are some of the more obvious 'don'ts' during pregnancy:

– Smoking during pregnancy means that your baby is likely to be born smaller than normal.

– Alcohol drinking during pregnancy, especially in large amounts, means that the baby does not grow so well and also can be brain damaged (the very occasional alcoholic drink in moderation is probably OK).

– The illegal drugs are all thought to affect unborn babies – but to varying degrees. The real bad ones are heroin and cocaine: babies whose mothers are addicted can get into all sorts of trouble, especially when they are born, as they get bad withdrawal symptoms. Almost all illegal drugs, including cannabis, affect people's brains, and the brains of developing babies inside the uterus (womb) are particularly sensitive.

Doc – **are there medicines that you shouldn't take during pregnancy?** 16 year old girl.

Dear 'Cautious about medicines in pregnancy' – Doctors usually advise trying to avoid taking any medicines, unless you have to have them (except folic acid and some vitamins, which should be taken in recommended amounts). If you are on medicines on a regular or even irregular basis and are even thinking of getting pregnant (which you should not be at your age!), check it out with your doctor, as even some antibiotics can cause problems.

Dear Doctor – **do drugs taken by the father have an effect on an unborn child?** 17 year old male.

Dear 'Concerned about effects of a father taking drugs – Yes, this is possible. Suppose the father was injecting heroin using dirty needles and syringes and he becomes infected with the HIV (Human immuno virus), then when he makes love to his wife/girlfriend she can become infected, and if she becomes pregnant and has the HIV virus in her bloodstream, this can then affect her unborn baby. But there are also concerns that alcohol, smoking and some drugs can affect the quality of a man's sperm.

Doctor Ann – **can you get HIV or AIDS from drugs?** 16 year old girl.

Dear 'HIV/AIDs enquirer' – The simple answer is yes you can, but only if you are (a) using a drug which you inject like heroin and (b) if you are using dirty equipment (needles and syringes already used by someone else) to do the injection with. HIV infections are not the only problem because you can get other nasty infections as well, including hepatitis from using dirty equipment. Because of this, in some places around the UK, needle exchange places have been set up where you can take your used syringes and needles and get clean ones in exchange. The trouble is that if you get the HIV virus, if you are pregnant, it will affect your unborn child. If you are having sexual relations with someone else or they are using your drug equipment, you are also a real danger to them.

● THE WORST END

Dear Doctor Ann – **can drugs kill you and how many people die from drugs?** 12 year old girl.

Dear 'Dead worried about drugs' – Yes, they certainly can. The most up-to-date reliable figures for deaths from drugs cover the period 1995 to 1999 for the population of England and Wales. During this five-year period, there were 227 deaths due to the use of cocaine, 213 deaths from the use of amphetamines, 78 deaths from ecstasy, 366 deaths from using solvents, 4743 deaths due to the use of morphine, heroin and other similar opiate drugs, 200,000 to 400,000 deaths due to alcohol, and over a million deaths due to the use of tobacco. All these deaths were theoretically avoidable, and devastation caused by such deaths is not only on the people who have died, but also on all these people's families, friends, workmates, etc.

Caffeine

The world's most popular drug?

TEA, COFFEE, COCOA AND COLAS - ARE THEY REALLY DRUGS?

Caffeine, along with tobacco, is one of the drugs most frequently used by human beings. It is present in many colas, as well as in tea, coffee and cocoa. One or two cups of coffee and four cups of tea contain enough caffeine to keep you feeling awake and alert for several hours. In the UK, we are said to drink over 120 million cups of tea a day – but who is counting?

● **MORE THAN YOUR ORDINARY CUPPA?**

Dear Dr ann – **we need some information on caffeine but it isn't anywhere. Is it a drug?** can you help? 14 year old girl.

Dear 'Concerned about caffeine' – Yes, caffeine is a drug and it is used in quite a wide variety of medicines, but it also occurs naturally in tea and coffee. Tea was actually originally sold in England as a medicine, rather than an everyday drink. Caffeine's chemical name is trimethylxanthine. In its pure form, it is a white crystalline powder that tastes very bitter. The chief source of pure caffeine is from the process of decaffeinating coffee and tea. Medically, it is used to stimulate people's hearts and for making them pee. Generally, it is also used as an 'energy booster' or for making people feel more alert. It is often used by students so that they can study late at night, and, for the same reason, by long-distance drivers. People do become addicted to caffeine in coffee or tea, and as a result, they feel that they 'cannot function' in the morning without a cup of coffee or tea. But it can also make their hearts beat faster and make them feel a bit jittery.

Dear Doc — my French girlfriend had a nervous breakdown because she was drinking ten cups of tea a day here and stopped when she went back to France. **I've heard that you can get addicted to caffeine – is it a drug and how much do you need to become an addict?** 16 year old boy.

Dear 'Boy with tea-drinking girlfriend' — Caffeine can be addictive. It seems to affect the same bits of the brain as cocaine, amphetamines and heroin, and in the same way, but the effects of caffeine are milder. Ground coffee contains about 140 mgs of caffeine per mug, and tea about 80 mgs, colas about 36 mgs per can, and chocolate about 6 mgs in a bar. Looking at it in this way, your girlfriend was probably consuming quite enough to get a bit addicted to it, especially if she felt that she couldn't do without it when she got back to France – or was it you she was addicted to and couldn't do without?

Dear Doc – **can I get caffeine in some sort of concentrate form to help me stay awake and concentrate when studying?** 16 year old boy.

Dear 'Concentrater' – There are various concentrated caffeine tablets available from chemists. Don't take more than the recommended dose. Taking too much caffeine can make you anxious and make your ability to concentrate and take in information worse. Getting a decent night's sleep and not using something like caffeine may be far better at helping you to study.

Some caffeine facts

- *The effects of caffeine take around an hour to come on and they last for 3–4 hours.*
- *Chronic coffee/tea drinkers (drinking more than 1000 mgs of caffeine a day) can get increased tiredness, headaches and irritability.*

Dr Ann – **how much coffee and tea can I drink to help keep me awake for studying for my exams?** 17 year old girl.

Dear 'Coffee/tea drinker' – People's tolerance to tea and coffee varies from one person to another. In general though, it is a delicate balance between having enough caffeine to have the 'wanted' effects of staying awake, and not taking so much that you have the 'unwanted' effects of becoming anxious and jumpy. Roughly two cups of ground coffee or four cups of instant coffee or tea every four hours should do the trick, so I am told – but it sounds rather a lot to me! But watch out for not being able to sleep at night, your heart beating faster, and becoming sweaty. The effects of caffeine in coffee and tea take about an hour to come on, and last for about three to four hours.

One cup of ground coffee has the same amount of caffeine as two mugs of instant coffee or tea, twenty mugs of cocoa, four mugs of coca cola, or six (100mgs) bars of chocolate.

QUIZ 1 HOW DRUGWISE ARE YOU?

1

Which of the following are drugs?
- a tobacco
- b cannabis
- c penicillin

2

Who does illegal drugs?
- a One out of five 15-year-olds do illegal drugs
- b After the age of 20, the older you are the more likely you are to do illegal drugs
- c Half of all 16-year-olds have been offered an illegal drug

3

Why do young people take drugs?
- a To find out what they are like
- b To be one of the crowd
- c Because they find it better than their 'real' lives

4

It is illegal to:
- a drink alcohol under the age of 16
- b sell cigarettes to a 15-year-old
- c be in possession of a tablet of ecstasy

5

Which of the following can you get dependent on?
- a caffeine
- b tobacco
- c cannabis

If you got them all right – then you are drugwise, which means that you are less likely to try drugs. If you got them all wrong – then you need to drugwise up quickly.

Answers

1 **a, b** and **c** are all correct, because they are all chemical substances which affect your body – even if they are not illegal

2 **a** and **c** are both correct. After 20, the older you are, the less likely you are to take drugs

3 **a, b** and **c** are all correct. However, the commonest reason is to 'find out what they are like'.

4 **b** and **c** are right. It is illegal to buy alcohol until you are 18 years old, though you can drink it before that age, e.g. in your own home

5 **a, b** and **c** are correct. Arguments about what 'dependency' means as against 'addiction', probably don't actually amount to very much.

7 Money

Up in smoke

Everyone knows that smoking is bad – even the tobacco companies who spend at least £100 million a year telling us how and what we should smoke. There are 4000 chemicals in each cigarette, and thousands of trees are destroyed to package the fags. 1000 million people will die from smoking in the 21st century. Eighty-four per cent of people who smoke wish they had never started. Smoking causes 50 different illnesses, 20 of them fatal, and nicotine is as addictive as heroin.

● THE WHY, THE WHO, THE COST

Dear Dr Ann – **WHY do people smoke? I just think it's plain retarded.** Boy aged 14.

Dear 'Puzzled non-smoker' –
People tend to try smoking for lots of

41

different reasons, but the main ones are:– because friends do it; because they think it makes them look 'hard'; to experiment and find out what it is like; to rebel and do something against authority; to look cool and sophisticated; to make themselves feel more self-confident; because they think it helps them concentrate; because they think that it helps keep them thin, and because cigarette companies, until the recent ban, advertised cigarettes to people in a way that was seductive and sexy. I agree that it's plain retarded to smoke, given what we know about the bad effects.

Hi *doc* – **why are there more teenage girl smokers than boys?** Girl aged 15.

Dear 'Why do so many girls smoke' – For a long time, smoking was considered a male problem. However, in 2001, 25% of girls and 19% of boys aged 15 smoked at least one cigarette a week, and of course, most of them smoked many more than one. It's difficult to know why women want to be even more stupid than men over smoking, especially as there are special risks for women as they get older and want children. Cigarette advertising was a factor, as tobacco companies have particularly targeted young women in recent years with subtle claims that it helps them keep slim.

Dear Dr ann – **My friend is 14 and she says she smokes because it makes her not eat so she has stayed thin – is this what is causing it?** Girl aged 15.

Dear 'Friend of a staying thin girl' — Lots of girls start smoking because they think it will help them get thin as well as make them sophisticated and sexy. Smoking doesn't make people thin – it just costs a lot of money, makes your breath smell bad, and gets you hooked onto something which is very, very hard to give up. Your friend won't suddenly turn into a whale if she stops smoking, though some people do put on a few pounds when they first quit, partly because after a few days food tastes nicer. Tell her she'll then tend to lose it again, though some people who have cigarettes for pudding instead of a cream cake do find the weight goes on when they go back to the cream cakes. Suggest she eats some fruit instead. Many people who give up smoking don't notice any weight change at all – their body adjusts happily. If your friend quits, she'll be looking better and feeling better, she'll smell better, and with the money she saves, she'll be able to afford to enrol in one of those classy gyms, keep slim and buy more clothes.

Dear Doctor Ann — **hiya! how old do u have to be b4 you can smoke?** Girl aged 13.

Dear 'Age b4 you can smoke' — You can smoke fags at any age, BUT you have to be 16 before you can go into a shop and buy cigarettes. Someone who sells cigarettes to anyone who is under 16 can be prosecuted. Unfortunately, many shopkeepers ignore this law, probably unintentionally because it can be very difficult to check out people's age unless they show an 'honest' means of identification. The older you are before you try fags, the less likely you are to be an 'always' smoker, and the more likely you are to be a 'never' smoker.

Dear Doctor Ann – **how many teenage smokers are there in an average class?** Boy aged 14.

> *Dear 'Wanting to know about number of teenage smokers' –*
> 'Too many' is the right answer. It also depends on the age of the teenagers in the class. In a class of pupils aged 15, one in four girls say they smoke cigarettes regularly and one in five boys say the same. Many more of the class will have tried a fag but not gone on smoking. If you are one of the ones who is smoking regularly – remember you could join in the bigger crowd and give it up!

● **SMOKING AND YOUR BODY**

Dear Dr Ann – **will the dentist know that you smoke?** 13 year old female.

> *Dear 'Wondering if dentists detect smokers' –*
> Probably, because of the smell when you open your mouth and s/he gets close to you. Also, if you smoke a lot, your teeth tend to get a bit discoloured from the tobacco, your gums get sore, swollen and red, causing your teeth to fall out earlier.

Dr ann – **People say smoking stops your penis from growing. Is this true?** Boy age 14.

> *Dear 'Worried about smoking and penis growth' –* Yes, it stops you growing hard, otherwise known as impotence, though it doesn't stop your

44

penis itself growing. It's been calculated that in the UK, there are 120,000 men under the age of 50 who are impotent (can't get their penis up whatever the size) because of smoking!

Dear Doctor Ann – **can I get ill if i have 1 fag a day if yes what can i get from it.** Age: 15 Sex: female.

> *Dear 'One fag a day person'* – We know that it is best to smoke no fags, and that even breathing in the smoke of others – called 'passive' smoking – can cause health problems, including chest infections and lung cancer when you are older. So best is no fags, but only one a day is much better than ten a day if you have to smoke (try not to inhale if you do smoke even just one). The trouble is that because the nicotine in cigarettes is so addictive, it is often difficult to stick to one a day.

Dear Doctor Ann – **what are the effects of smoking? are there any positive effects?** Boy age 14.

> *Dear 'What are the good effects of smoking'* – It would be stupid to pretend there are no good effects as most people smoke because they enjoy it. However, few people enjoy their first cigarette and often feel sick and a sense of choking. Most people like smoking because they say it helps them relax and concentrate. Unfortunately, the bad effects of smoking (including the risk of heart disease, lung cancer, fewer sperm, making you smell) far outweigh the good effects, especially as the nicotine is so addictive.

GOING DOWN IN SMOKE

Dear Dr Ann — **How do fags kill you?** boy age 13.

Dear 'How do fags kill you' — There are several different ways that fags kill you. Lung cancer is the best known one, but there are lots of other nasty deadly diseases caused by the habit. The list is endless: heart disease, heart attacks, high blood pressure, brain haemorrhages, cancer of the lip, cancer of the oesophagus, cancer of the cervix, and a lung disease called emphysema, to name but a few. For young women, smoking also increases the risk of having a heart attack if they are on the contraceptive pill. Out of 1000 people who smoke, 500 will die from smoking tobacco and are more likely to die in their forties than in old age.

Dear Doctor Ann — **how long does smoking take off your life?** Girl aged 16.

Dear 'Shorter life' — Every cigarette you smoke, on average, knocks five minutes off your life. Half of all smokers eventually get killed by the tobacco they smoke. The half who don't get killed by tobacco may still get nasty coughs and splutters, as well as polluting other people's air. The half who do get killed by tobacco lose, on average, 16 years of their life. But if you smoke and you manage to stop by the age of 20, then you don't run any increased risk of dying, and if you stop before the age of 30, you avoid over 90% of the tobacco-induced lung cancer risk. So the sooner you give up, the safer and easier it is.

● **TRYING TO STOP**

Dear Dr Ann — **I have tried to stop smoking but all my so called friends keep bullying me to carry on.** Girl aged 16.

> **Dear 'Wanting to quit smoker'** — You're right to call them 'so-called' friends. Unfortunately, people often want support for their own bad habits by getting or keeping other people involved to make themselves feel better. Find a mate who does want to give up – doing it with someone else often helps. The following might help you go about it:
> • Pick a day together to stop smoking.
> • Report to each other every day about how you are doing.
> • Work out a list of things to do instead of smoking when you feel like having one.
> • Consider using nicotine gum or patches.
> • Avoid the friends who want to push you into having a fag until you feel you have really quit.
> • Give yourselves a treat each week or month with the money you have saved. You'll both deserve it.

Dear Doctor Ann — **if I try smoking will I get addicted straight away?** 15 year old boy.

Dear 'Wondering how quickly you can get addicted to fags' — Everyone is different, but some people feel they are hooked after as few as three to five fags, while others need more. It's even been said that nicotine in cigarettes is at least as addictive as heroin, and we know that is very addictive — so it's best NOT to try either of them. Remember, if you do get hooked on tobacco, you can still give up — it is never too late to give up and the sooner you try to the better. There are lots of ways to get help.

THE PASSIVE SMOKING SCENE

Dear Doctor Ann — **Both my parents smoke and i hate it what should i do?** Worried child age 13.

Dear 'Girl with smoking parents' — Unfortunately, smoking cigarettes is very addictive. People only give up when they really want to and often need help by using nicotine patches or gum. You could suggest they try these as they can be bought from any chemist. You've probably already tried nagging them, hiding their fags or making rude remarks about the smell and it hasn't worked? You could try a serious discussion about your worries about the dangers of smoking for them, and of passive smoking, and get them to agree not to smoke in certain rooms in the house when you are all together. Meanwhile, carry on hating smoking and don't take it up yourself. Let them know that their smoking also puts others at risk. Every year in the UK, there are 17,000 children admitted to hospital and an estimated 300 deaths from passive smoking, from inhaling the cigarette smoke from others smoking.

Under the influence…
and out
of control

ALCOHOL AND WHAT IT DOES TO YOU AND YOUR BRAIN

Alcohol comes in many different forms of drink. All alcohol consists of the chemical ethanol, which can be made by the process of fermentation from a variety of things like grapes (wine), apples (cider), hops and barley (beer), rice (the Japanese drink *sake*) and a host of other plants and berries, including potatoes and flowers.

● **THE LAW, THE LIMITS, THE LIQUOR**

Dear Dr Ann — **why is it illegal for under 18s to drink?** Girl aged 16.

Dear 'Under 18' — In fact there is no law to say that people under 18 cannot drink alcohol — they can drink alcohol, but they are restricted as to where they can do this. The law states that people under 18 cannot buy an alcoholic drink or drink alcohol in the licensed part of a pub. Nor can they buy alcohol legally from supermarkets or off-licences. Most young people have their first alcoholic drink at about the age of 13 in their own homes with their parents.

Dear Doctor Ann — **what is the limit of alcohol you should drink?** 14 year old male.

Dear 'Wanting to know how much alcohol to drink — There are few 'shoulds' and lots of 'should nots' about drinking alcohol. In small amounts, alcohol can be great at relaxing you and making parties go with a bang, and may even be good for your health when you are older. So, almost no one is saying don't drink at all, except for some religious groups. It is the quantity that is important – this should probably be no more than two or three units in a day, and not every day when you are 14. Remember – a unit is HALF a pint of lager, not a pint! Adult males in this sexist world can manage 21 units a week, and adult females 14 units, but if you're under 18, the weekly intake should be less than this. Any more and you're doing damage to yourself. It may sound a bit sexist, but it's just nature as boys have more water and less fat in their bodies, so they can dilute the alcohol faster. Some young people are drinking too much, and this is not only damaging their livers but also getting them involved in accidents.

Dear Dr Ann — **do some people get more drunk than others easier?** Boy age 15.

Dear 'Do some get more easily drunk than others' — Unfortunately, it's an unfair world in lots of ways and that includes how much you can drink without feeling bad. We are all different in how tall or fat we are, and similarly the enzymes that break down the alcohol in our bodies also vary. It does seem that the more you drink, the more enzymes your liver produces, but that's not a good reason to drink too much, as after a certain amount of alcohol everyone gets drunk. And of course, if you are a boy, you can drink a bit more than a girl before you get drunk.

Dear Doctor Ann — **How many units are there in 8 pints of beer?** Boy age 15.

Dear 'Unit measurer' — Each pint has two units, so your answer is 16. You certainly should not be drinking this much in an evening as you will get very drunk and very, very ill. In fact, eight pints is more than you should be drinking in a whole week if you are under 18, whether you are a boy or a girl, and certainly not all in one go. This kind of drinking is known as binge drinking.

Dear Doctor Ann — **What is the % alcohol in beer?** 13 male.

Dear 'Percentage in beer person' — Different beers have different percentage of alcohol. Standard beer and lager have 3.5% alcohol, whereas premium beer and lager have 5%. Watch out for the super strength lager, which is 9%, which means you would get drunk much quicker with drinking the same amount. Other drinks also vary in the percentage of alcohol. Most wines have one part of alcohol to eight parts of water, and some spirits have as much as one part of alcohol to two parts of water. The higher the percentage of alcohol in a drink, the less you will need before you get drunk.

Dear Dr Ann – **I'm 16 and i feel that i get left behind when I'm out with my friends and go to the pub** because when we sit down and have a drink my friends are usually on their 2nd or 3rd when I've finished my 1st.

Dear 'Slow drinker' – **Don't be tempted to go with the pack. It sounds as though your pattern of drinking is the better model – you're less likely to get drunk, less likely to have a hangover and you'll have more money to spend on other things. Drink isn't cheap, and after you've spent a lot of money on it, the only thing you are left with is a bad hangover and feeling really ill.**

One unit = half a pint of beer
            = 1 glass of wine
            = a small glass of sherry
            = less than half a pint of cider

If you're very drunk at night, you may still be over the limit the next morning.

You're four times more likely to have an accident on your bike if you've had alcohol to drink, and you can be prosecuted for being drunk in charge of a bicycle.

One in five people killed in road accidents is over the limit.

Dear Doctor Ann — **What are the health risks to drinking alcohol??** Age:15 female.

Dear 'Wanting to know about alcohol' — The main health risk from alcohol to someone your age is drinking too much, getting drunk and having an accident or getting into a fight. Around half of all pedestrians aged 16 to 60 who are killed in road accidents in the UK have more booze in their bloodstream than the legal drink-drive limit. Not to mention those hurt in the car. And it's not just car accidents. Alcohol starts by relaxing you but ends up making you lose your self-control and your judgement. You then drink more, get into fights, or into bed with no contraception with someone you don't really like.

Dear Dr Ann — **when you drink alcohol wot part of you is it affecting and which body organ processes the alcohol??** Boy age 12.

Dear 'What does alcohol do to your body' — When you have an alcoholic drink, it quickly gets absorbed from your stomach into the bloodstream. The alcohol gets to circulate around your body and into every cell. It affects your brain within five to ten minutes so that you feel relaxed and less inhibited (less shy). A small amount makes people feel more lively and relaxed about life, but a larger amount can do the opposite. If you really drink too much in one go, you can become unconscious because of the effect on the brain. There are lots of problems caused by drinking too much alcohol over a long time – it inflames and scars your liver (the organ that processes the alcohol you drink) so the cells don't work, gives you bleeding and ulcers in the stomach, cancer of the mouth and throat, and can make you depressed or mentally ill. And if you are female, drinking a lot during pregnancy can make the baby be born brain-damaged or very small.

Dear Doctor Ann – **Since I have been going out with my new boyfriend I have been getting very stressed and so have found myself drinking a large amount on occasions,** what can I do to calm me down? And is it because of my new boyfriend?
Age: 15 female.

Dear 'Getting stressed and drinking too much' – Is there something about this new relationship that is making you feel stressed so that you are using drink to cope with the stress? Unfortunately, drinking too much alcohol is not going to help your stress, though it may appear to make you feel more confident. Sit down and write down just how much you are drinking, and when and why, so as to try and sort out what is really happening. The best way to find something to calm you down is to find out what is making you stressed. Then you can deal with the cause, and that might mean changing the new boyfriend?

Dear Doctor Ann – I think I'm really fat and ugly. I weigh about 8 stone and I'm about 5ft 7 inches I started making myself sick about a year ago and now i can't stop. I've now moved onto alcohol to make me feel better. I see a counsellor but things aren't improving. I'm getting worse and I'm isolating myself and having trouble with sleeping. please help me. What's wrong with me? Age:16 Sex: female.

Dear 'Person who thinks she is fat and ugly but is NOT' — There's no way that you could be overweight if you only weigh 8 stone, but it does sound like you are depressed and have bulimia, which is the name for the vomiting you are doing. Please, please tell your counsellor how you are feeling, as you may need more help – possibly from a doctor who is a specialist in depression, called a psychiatrist. Sometimes antidepressant pills may help. But remember, the alcohol will only make things worse as it tends to make people more depressed. Although you don't have a weight problem, the alcohol wouldn't help someone who did, as every glass of wine contains 80 calories, and some pints of beer have as many calories as a Mars bar.

Dear Doctor Ann — **why should one 'not drink alcohol' while taking antibiotics?** Does it lessen the effect of the antibiotic? Or increase the effect of the alcohol? or both? or what? Do 1 or 2 glasses of wine have much effect? and does it matter which type of alcohol? Girl aged 15.

Dear 'Person wanting to know about antibiotics and alcohol' — A very good question, which I had to check out myself! Well, I think I have some good news for you (and for myself!). In fact, contrary to popular belief, there is not much evidence that you should never drink whilst taking antibiotics. So one or two glasses will not have much effect, but too many glasses is not good for you whether you are taking antibiotics or not!

Dear dr Ann – **What is the bestest cure for a hangover?** girl age 15.

Dear 'Hangover girl' – I'm afraid there aren't any shortcuts, but drinking water whilst drinking alcohol will help stop the dehydration and two paracetamol should deal with the headache. It's a myth that black coffee, showers, a fry-up or more drink help – there's no way to sober up quickly. In general, it takes the body at least one hour to get rid of each unit of alcohol. You're probably feeling awful because your liver's exhausted from processing all that alcohol and your head's all dried out.

Dear Doctor Ann – **I'm a 10 year old boy and one day i got a bit overboard with sneaking some wine and drank a whole bottle – this was about 2 months ago but i still feel really really ill is it alcohol poisoning?**

Dear 'Wine sneaker' – I'm sure drinking a bottle of wine would have made you feel extremely rough with a hangover the next day or even the day after that. In fact, drinking that amount of alcohol in one night could be very dangerous because of the effect on your brain. This amount of alcohol drunk at one go could even kill you by suppressing the breathing centre in your brain or making you vomit and the vomit getting into your lungs. However, as long as this does not happen, your body – mainly your liver – will have got rid of all the alcohol after a few days. There must be another reason for you feeling ill. If it's been going on for two months, it's time to check things out with your doctor.

● DO YOU GET DRUNKEN PARTS?

Dear Doc – **does drinking affect whether or not u will have sex?** Boy age 15.

Dear 'Potential drinking sex fiend' – Shakespeare said (and he should know a thing or two about it) that alcohol 'increaseth the desire and decreaseth the performance'. This poor performance is due to difficulties in getting an erection (also known as 'brewer's droop'!) The main problem with alcohol is that it removes people's normal controls and upsets their judgement about sensible things to do and not to do. Research shows that a considerable number of people who have sex for the first time do it whilst under the influence of alcohol, and regret it later.

9 Cannabis –

please at least know this much

Cannabis is the illegal drug that is most widely used by young people in the UK. A survey carried out in 2000 showed that around 2 million people in the UK are occasional users of the drug, and that just over half of all young men aged 16 to 24 and just under half of all young women of the same age, have tried it. About one in five young people had used cannabis in the last year, and one in twelve have used it in the last month.

● THE EFFECTS

Doc – **why do people smoke 'weed'?** 17 year old boy.

Dear 'Wondering why people smoke the weed' – Mainly because of the effects that cannabis has on how the brain 'sees' the outside world. The easiest way to describe these is feeling 'different'. But people who smoke cannabis say a great many other things about its effects, like 'everything becomes slightly unreal', 'it's as if everything is a little bit further away than normal', 'it makes me feel mellow', 'it makes things like taste and sound much, much more immediate but at the same time kind of distorted', 'everything in life seems stronger and pleasanter', 'makes me much less stressed', 'makes me relax when I am with other people'.

Doctor Ann — **what happens when you smoke weed?** 14 year old girl.

Dear 'Curious about the effects of weed' — Cannabis, or weed, contains more than 400 chemicals. Cannabis is normally smoked, and therefore gets into the body by being inhaled into the lungs. From the inside of the lungs the drugs are transferred to the bloodstream across the walls of the tiny sacs of the lungs called 'alveoli'. In the bloodstream these chemicals are then carried around your body up to the cells of your brain, where they have their effect. The inhaled chemical from cannabis that has most effect is called delta-9-tetrahydrocannobinol (THC) and different types of cannabis contain different amounts of THC.

Taking cannabis also decreases your blood pressure, increases your pulse rate, can give you bloodshot eyes, tends to increase appetite, and some people get dizziness. Effects of smoking cannabis start within a few minutes and may last several hours or longer. When eaten, the effects take longer to start but may last much longer as well.

Dear Dr Ann — **are there any good effects on your body from smoking weed?** 16 year old boy.

Dear 'Good effects of 'weed' smoking' — Smoking cannabis makes people feel relaxed, and if they are in a good mood before they smoke the drug, then this feeling is usually reinforced by the cannabis itself. Other positive effects of the drug include helping people sleep, helping people feel better if they have an incurable illness like multiple sclerosis, and helping with the feelings of sickness brought on by some other chemical substances used in the treatment of cancer. Because of these beneficial effects, scientists are now allowed to do research on the cannaboid chemicals derived from cannabis – but only under very strict research conditions.

Dear Dr ann — **is cannabis safe to smoke?** 15 year old boy.

Dear 'Is cannabis safe person' — What is your definition of 'safe'? Let me give you the facts. Cannabis is not safe because you can still get arrested for using it. It is not safe because it contains cancerous chemicals, it is not safe because it is associated with an increased chance of you getting depression (nasty) and schizophrenia (nastier). But remember

that neither smoking tobacco or drinking alcohol is 'completely safe', or for that matter driving a car! Most of life has risks attached to it, but I would NOT want to risk getting arrested – and I wouldn't want ANY of the bad effects of cannabis either.

Doctor – **can you help me? How much cannabis can I smoke. Can you smoke too much weed.** 14 year old boy.

> *Dear 'Can I smoke too much weed'* – Most responsible adults would say that smoking 'any' cannabis is smoking too much. But given that about half the population of teenagers will try cannabis (as have many, many 'responsible' adults), I am taking your question a bit further. The more 'weed' that you smoke, the more chance you have of getting problems such as demotivation (not wanting to do anything), depression, memory loss, schizophrenia, dependency on the drug, and lung troubles, not just from the cannabis, but also from the tobacco which most people tend to smoke it with. Most of these things are 'dose-related', meaning the more you have, the greater the chances are that you will have a problem. So the less that you smoke the better, and yes – none is best of all!

Hi Doc Ann – **I smoke cannabis and I'm just wondering I feel more tired/worn out at skool could you tell me if this is because of the cannabis or jus lack of sleep** I tend to go to bed around 11.30 and wake up around 7.00 thanx ANON (so solid kru 4eva) 14 year old boy.

> *Dear 'Worn-out cannabis smoker'* – The answer is that you may be tired from many different things – like stress, finding the money to pay for your cannabis, lack of sleep, etc. But, but, but... yes, you may well be tired because of smoking cannabis as well. Cannabis can have effects lasting days, and its effects do tend to 'build up'.

Doctor Ann — **what are the other names for weed?** 14 year old girl.

Dear 'Weed word searcher' — There are hundreds of names for cannabis and these increase all the time. Some of these names depend on the form of the cannabis – hash, resin, grass, weed, etc. Other names depend on how it is smoked – spliff, joint, jay, reefer, etc. Some names are just names like dope, shit, draw, pot, gear, puff. Some names are from the 'East', like dagga, kabak, charas, bhang, ganga, etc. Some names are new forms of cannabis, like all the names for 'skunk', which is a hybrid form of cannabis, and include names like 'white widow', 'purple haze', 'California orange'. There are also some comic names like 'Henry VIII'.

Doctor — **Can you tell me what does cannabis look like?** 13 year old boy.

Dear 'Wondering what cannabis looks like' — Cannabis comes in several different forms. There is the whole cannabis plant, which looks something like the plant in this chapter. Cannabis resin is a light or dark greenish-brown substance, which is obtained by scraping it off the surface of the cannabis plant. It comes in hard lumps. Cannabis oil is a treacly liquid.

Dear Ann — **what is the history of cannabis?** 14 year old boy.

Dear 'Curious about cannabis's past' — The first mention of cannabis is when it was used as medicine in Egypt around 3600 years ago. The Chinese were growing it around 2400 years ago for medicinal purposes. The drug was brought to Western Europe by soldiers in Napoleon's army who had been fighting in North Africa at the beginning of the 19th century. Cannabis did not really become popular for its 'mind-altering properties' in England until sometime in the 1800s, when it was used by artists and intellectuals. But it wasn't until 50 years ago that it really began to be used extensively in the UK, when it was imported from Jamaica as a 'fun' drug. Although it is known to have medicinal effects, such as its painkilling properties, its help in suppressing vomiting, and as a sleep-inducing drug, the use of cannabis was banned in the UK in 1928. Arguments about whether it should be legal or not have raged ever since.

● **TESTING POSITIVE... 1, 2, 3, 4 DAYS OR MORE?**

Dr Ann — **can you test positively for marijuana after eating it rather than inhaling it?** 17 year old girl.

Dear 'Ingester of cannabis' — Whether you inhale it or eat it, the drug ends up in your bloodstream, either by absorption across the walls of your lungs or across the walls of your intestine. It is then carried in your blood up to the brain where it has its effect. Your blood gets rid of the chemicals that are in cannabis into your pee. Tests for cannabis can be done on your hair, blood and urine. But for all these tests the answer is yes — whether you smoke it or eat it, you can test positive for it.

Dear Dr Ann — **How long does cannabis take to get out your system?** 15 year old boy.

Dear 'Wanting to get rid of cannabis' – This will depend on what you mean by 'out of your system'. If you mean how long does one go on feeling the effects of cannabis after taking it, the answer depends on the individual. There is no doubt that some people go on feeling 'funny' after smoking cannabis for 24 hours or more. If, on the other hand, you are asking the question 'how long after taking cannabis could I still test positive for the drug if I had a blood or urine test', then the answer for cannabis is two to seven days, but up to a month for regular users – and it can also be detected for up to three months in your hair.

Using the weed:
The myths
and the
problems

There are almost as many myths as actual certainties about the good and bad effects of using cannabis. There is, however, an increasing amount of scientific research on the drug because it does seem to have some medicinal properties, like decreasing the side effects of some cancer therapies. But there is also increasing evidence that it does also have bad effects on the brain. However, sorting out what is myth and what is fact can still be difficult!

● EFFECTS ON BODY GROWTH

Dr Ann – **does smoking weed affect your love life?** 16 year old boy.

Dear 'Does weed affect your love life' – Well, where do you want me to begin? Some male cannabis users do find that they have greater difficulties getting an erection when they are using the weed. Cannabis, whether you smoke it or take it by mouth in some form or other (like in hash brownies), can also change your behaviour so that you do things that you wouldn't normally do. An example might be getting into sexual situations you later regret, or forgetting to use condoms or other forms of contraception that you would normally use. Finally, cannabis alters the way that you sense the world – it sensitises your taste sensations and your perception of music, etc. So it may also change the way that you feel about sex – either for better or for worse!

Dear Dr Ann – **does smoking weed decrease the size of your penis?** 15 male.

> *Dear 'Male wondering about the effects of weed on his penis' –* There's no evidence that it makes your penis smaller – or bigger for that matter – though some guys complain that it makes it more difficult to get an erection.

Dr ann – **can weed make you temporarily infertile?** 17 year old girl.

> *Dear 'Worried about weed making you infertile' –* I really can't answer this one because I don't think anyone has really researched it. But I certainly would NOT recommend that you ever consider the idea of using it as a form of contraception! Cannabis can certainly make you less inhibited in your sexual behaviour, so you may need to actually increase your concentration on using contraception if you are going to

smoke cannabis and have sex at the same time. What we do know is that smoking *tobacco* does have an effect on *men's* fertility, and as most people smoke cannabis with tobacco, it probably does have some effect on men's sperm production!

Dear Dr Ann – **is it true that weed stunts your growth if you haven't fully grown?** 16 year old boy.

Dear 'Worried about the weed stunting growth' – No one has, as far as I know, ever looked to see if cannabis by itself does or doesn't stunt a person's growth. Smoking cigarettes stunts your growth though, because tobacco affects your lungs so that the amount of oxygen that gets into your bloodstream is less when you smoke cigarettes, and oxygen is one of the rather essential things that you need to live and grow. Most people smoke cannabis with tobacco, so you can draw your own conclusions!

● **IF IT'S A MEDICINE, IS IT HARMLESS?**

Dear Doctor Ann – **my mum had breast cancer, and when she had to have medicines to treat it, she said that she was given something made of cannabis to help her feel better? Is this true?** 15 year old girl.

Dear 'Mum with breast cancer' – I do hope that your mother is OK. Yes, it is possible that she was given a synthetic cannabis extract called nabilone because it is sometimes used

legally as a medicine nowadays to suppress some of the more unpleasant side effects of the chemicals used in the treatment of cancer. The beneficial medical effects of cannabis have been recognized for thousands of years, and at the moment, are particularly recognized by people suffering from diseases such as multiple sclerosis. At last, the medical profession is being allowed to carry out proper research on the medicinal effects of the drug – so now we'll really know about whether it is a useful medicine or not.

Cannabis was used by the Chinese over 1900 years ago as a herbal remedy and since then it has been widely used in the Middle East and India as a medicine. The use of cannabis for pleasure also dates back to ancient China and India.

Doc – my boyfriend smokes a lot of weed. He says its OK because he uses herbs and they can't give you lung cancer is it true?
16 year old girl.

Dear 'Person with boyfriend smoking weed' – Absolutely NOT true. The idea that so-called 'herbs' can only do you good is a total myth, I am afraid. Cannabis contains a large number of chemical substances, which do all sorts of things to you, as well as blowing your mind. Many of these chemical substances can also cause cancer, just as tobacco does. But you could also remind him of the other side effects of smoking cannabis – like a greater chance of developing schizophrenia or depression.

Doc — I need some helpful information about smoking cannabis. My friends smoke it and they never seem to have any side effects but all the websites about drugs say that there are side effects. 14 year old girl.

Dear 'Girl with friends who smoke cannabis' – If you smoke cigarettes, there are no apparent side effects when you are doing the actual smoking, but millions and millions of people around the world are dying because of the long-term effects of smoking tobacco. It is not surprising, therefore, that when your friends smoke cannabis, they don't seem to have side effects. However, cannabis actually contains chemicals which do all sorts of things to your body. Some of these have an effect straight away, for example increasing your heart rate and your blood pressure. Then there are the effects on how your brain 'sees' the world – this can be fairly profoundly changed. Another effect is increasing forgetfulness, and then there are the effects on your lungs, because smoking cannabis can, in the very long run, cause cancer (see also Chapter 11). What is most important for you to know is that the side effects of cannabis are usually dose-related, so that the more you smoke, the more likely you are to get harmful effects.

Dear Doc — is it safe to smoke it on one off occasions or will my parents know when i have done it? 15 year old girl.

Dear 'Secretive cannabis smoker' – Well, the obvious things to parents are the very characteristic smell of cannabis when it is smoked, and also their children acting

'dopey', and maybe your guilty look. Unfortunately for the children, most parents seem to have an awful 'instinct' for what their children are up to, though some may sometimes choose to turn a blind eye!

Hey Ann – **i was just wondering if it's dangerous to smoke weed as well as drinking a little bit of alcohol.** 15 year old boy.

Dear 'Weeder and drinker' – Interestingly enough, young people seem to know that drinking and smoking the weed is NOT a good idea and therefore tend NOT to mix the two. There has, over recent years, been regular testing of people who have been involved in car accidents, and the number of people with evidence of having the weed as well as alcohol in their blood has increased enormously. Drugs like cannabis are known to impair driving ability, though it can affect different people in different ways. But mixing alcohol and cannabis is certainly more dangerous in affecting your behaviour so that you are less in control of things, than just using one of the two at a time.

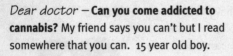

● IS CANNABIS ADDICTIVE AND CAN IT KILL?

Dear doctor – **Can you come addicted to cannabis?** My friend says you can't but I read somewhere that you can. 15 year old boy.

Dear 'Becoming addicted to cannabis' – Physical addiction or dependency on cannabis is virtually unknown. However, 'mental' addiction or dependency on it, if you are using it regularly, is well known. The bad effects of cannabis are dose-related, so the more you smoke it the worse the side effects are.

Dear Ann – **my best friend smokes cannabis. I am really worried about her. Can she get ill or die?** 14 year old girl.

Dear 'Worried about best friend' – You can stop worrying about your friend dying directly as a result of smoking cannabis – that is not a problem. As for getting ill from smoking cannabis, most people smoke cannabis without getting ill because they only do it occasionally and stop smoking it in their twenties. A very occasional person finds that it makes them sick. But it can also make people depressed, moody, demotivated and cause serious mental health problems. However, people who smoke cannabis tend to inhale it more deeply and for longer than those who smoke tobacco alone. So both the cannabis and the tobacco are in contact with the lungs for longer and therefore the risks of cancer are increased.

11 Don't do it
but if you do, use knowledge

There is no getting away from the fact that cannabis, whether you smoke it or take it by mouth, does have some bad effects. You can argue whether these effects are better or worse, or more or less likely to occur than, for example, when smoking tobacco or drinking alcohol. What you can't argue about is that these bad effects of cannabis exist. It is also a fact that, in general, the more cannabis you use, the more likely you are to get the bad effects.

● **DON'T RUIN YOUR BODY, BRAIN OR BABY**

Dr Ann — **what are the immediate effects of cannabis on you?** 14 year old boy.

Dear 'Immediate effects of cannabis enquirer' – Well, if you

72

use a lot... you begin to... oh, yeah... sort of... umh... forget things; you lose your, what is it called? That thing... um, er... concentration. This can give you trouble with your schoolwork and your social life. In fact, you can become a real dopehead. If you are a person who tends to get a bit depressed or anxious anyhow, then there are forms of cannabis – one called 'skunk' because it stinks, and another called 'chaos' for obvious reasons – which may make things worse and can make you sleepless, bad-tempered, and not nice to know at all. A small number of people are particularly vulnerable to mental health problems, and for them, cannabis may bring on a mental illness like schizophrenia or depression.

Dear Doc – **my Dad's a doctor and he says that I shouldn't smoke the weed because it can make me mad. Is there any truth in what he says?** I daren't ask him because then he'd know that I smoked. 15 year old boy.

Dear 'Secretive cannabis smoker with doctor Dad' – Yes, I think your dad is right and has been reading his medical journals because there has been a whole lot about this in one of the medical journals just recently. There are basically two serious mental health problems associated with smoking cannabis. Firstly, the chances of you getting schizophrenia (going mad) appear to be six times higher if you smoke cannabis than if you don't. It is not yet clear whether smoking cannabis makes it more likely that someone who has a tendency to get schizophrenia actually gets it, or whether cannabis actually causes schizophrenia. But the more you smoke, the more likely you are to get schizophrenia. There does also appear to be a link between depression and smoking cannabis, but this is less obvious.

Dear Dr ann — **my friend has quit smoking cannabis because it left her feeling down all the time. Will she eventually get back to herself.** After 3–4 months it must be out of her system so if she gave it up this long could it look a lot better for her in the next few months? 15 year old girl.

Dear 'Girl with friend who has given up cannabis' – Smoking cannabis has the strange effect of strengthening the mood that you were in when you started to smoke it. So, if your friend has a tendency to be depressed, then smoking cannabis will have been making it worse. It may actually cause people to get depressed. The best thing that you can do is to be there for your friend and listen to her troubles (telling someone else about what one finds depressing is a help by itself). Smoking cannabis certainly won't help her get rid of her feelings of depression but just make them worse.

Dear Ann — **I'm v. worried 'cos my sister is pregnant and i know she smokes weed – will it harm her baby?** Girl aged 15.

Dear 'Worried sister' – Smoking anything during pregnancy is a very bad idea – whether it is cannabis, tobacco or anything else. During the early development of a baby inside their mother, the baby is extremely vulnerable to any nasty things in their mother's bloodstream, and that includes both medical drugs and illegal drugs. See if you can persuade your sister to stop smoking either tobacco or cannabis, or both, as it will be doing her baby harm.

Dear Doctor Ann – **can it be harmful to use marijuana and prescription drugs?** Age: 17 Sex: male.

Dear 'Wanting to know about marijuana and prescription drugs' – It very much depends on which prescription drugs you are talking about. If it is any of the antidepressants, it can be extremely harmful.

● **MONEY, THE DEALERS AND THE POLICE**

Dr ann – **hello I have a fat drug habit – can you help – I smoke too much weed and I am always in debt – help.** 15 year old boy.

Dear 'Boy with a fat drug habit' – Being broke all the time is a very common side effect of smoking cannabis. People mention the incredibly high cost of smoking fags – a pack of 20 a day can set you back £1500 a year. But if you add on to that the cost of feeding yourself with marijuana at the same time, then the costs can more than double! Best to give up the fags and the marijuana and be richer by an incredible amount that could pay for DVD players, CDs, gameboys – you name it.

Watch out though, because most people find the tobacco harder to give up than the marijuana, because tobacco is very addictive – much more so than the weed.

Dear Dr Ann – **does smoking cannabis mean you get on to worse stuff?** 15 year old girl.

> *Dear 'Worried about worse stuff'* –
> No, taking cannabis does not *necessarily* mean that you will go on to other drugs. It is just that obtaining cannabis sometimes brings you into direct contact with people who 'deal' in drugs. They may try and push you into trying other illegal, more dangerous and more addictive drugs such as crack or heroin so that they will make more money out of you.

Dear Dr Ann – **just how unlawful is cannabis?** 14 year old boy.

> *Dear 'Cannabis and the law enquirer'* – Cannabis is (whether you like it or not) illegal and will stay illegal. At the present time though, it is being changed from being a class B drug, where you can get five years and a fine for possessing the drug, and 14 years plus a fine for dealing in the drug. It is being changed to a class C drug, which means that the maximum prison sentence you can get for possession is two years, and that you can get five years in prison for dealing.

● **TOBACCO, CANNABIS, CANCER AND ADDICTION**

Hi dr ann – **just wondering does weed have the same effect as a cigarette on your lungs??** 16 year old girl.

Dear 'Wondering about the weed's effect on the lungs' – The answer is pretty horrid, I am afraid. Cannabis, like tobacco (and mostly they are smoked together), damages the lining of the lung. Two to three cannabis cigarettes a day are the equivalent to 15 or more tobacco cigarettes in this respect. The amounts of cancer-causing chemicals in cannabis smoke are higher than those in cigarettes and the only reason why more people don't die of cancer from smoking cannabis is that they tend to smoke it less than cigarettes (fewer spliffs and for a shorter part of their lifetime).

Hey doc – **I'm worried that I am becoming addicted to cannabis is this possible?** i get moody and snappy when i haven't had a joint. I'm also worried that i am smoking it too much as i seem 2 be sharing at least 1 spliff a day with my friend is this going 2 damage me seriously? Boy age 14.

Dear 'Possible cannabis addict' – I think you already know you are smoking too much of this stuff without reading my reply. Don't carry on and become a 'dopehead', even though your friend wants to carry on sharing a spliff. Even if people tell you that you can't be addicted to cannabis, you can certainly become mentally dependent on it. I bet your moods will get better and you'll stop being so snappy a few days after you give it up. As for serious damage, we do know how cannabis affects your health in the long run as it contains lots of cancer chemicals. But you will also certainly be addicted to the nicotine you smoke the cannabis with – which means being hooked on fags long term. Long term use of tobacco causes cancer, bronchitis and heart disease.

QUIZ 2 TRUTHS AND LIES ABOUT ALCOHOL, SMOKING AND CANNABIS

1

One unit of alcohol is contained in:
- ☐ a a glass of wine
- ☐ b a pint of beer
- ☐ c a cocktail

2

The following are true of tobacco:
- ☐ a it is highly addictive
- ☐ b it causes heart disease
- ☐ c smoke from it is harmless to other people

3

It is illegal to:
- ☐ a buy tobacco under the age of 16
- ☐ b smoke tobacco under the age of 16
- ☐ c buy alcohol under the age of 18

4

The following is true of cannabis:
- ☐ a it affects your short-term memory
- ☐ b it is the most commonly used illegal drug in the UK
- ☐ c it is never associated with mental illness in people

5

Smoking cannabis is:
- ☐ a legal
- ☐ b harmless
- ☐ c the only way that cannabis is used

If you got them all right – you'll know that these drugs need treating with great caution.

If you have got them all wrong, re-read the first 12 chapters of the book and try again.

Answers

1: **a** is correct. A pint of beer is two units, and it is usually impossible to know how much alcohol there is in an average cocktail because it varies so much

2: **a** and **b** are correct. Passive smoking from other people smoking does harm other people's health.

3: **a** and **c** are correct – and although **b** isn't

4: **a** and **b** are correct. Some long-term users of cannabis do develop a mental illness

5: None of these are correct. Cannabis is still illegal but is being made into a class C drug, which means that you can get arrested, put into prison and fined for possession and dealing.

Inhaling,
sniffing and
popping

There are some drugs which people 'inhale' or 'sniff' rather than taking by mouth or injecting. The use of 'solvents' of one kind or another was popular in the 1970s and 1980s. Their use has gradually declined with the availability of ecstasy. Some of these solvents can cause sudden death, and between 70 and 100 young people in the UK are still **dying** from solvent-sniffing every year.

● **DISSOLVING IN SOLVENTS**

Dear Dr A – **What are solvents?** 15 year old girl.

Dear 'Inquisitive about solvents' – These are substances like nail varnish removers, aerosols, liquid-correcting fluid, glue, butane gas, and a whole range of household cleaners. People sniff them because they contain things called 'volatile hydrocarbons'. The effects are that they make you light-headed, 'drunk' and take away your inhibitions. These effects come on almost instantly and last around 15 to 45 minutes. Although solvents are something that we use in everyday life, when you sniff them in the high concentration, they are very dangerous. Used for the purpose they are designed for, they are fine, but they are not for sniffing!

Doc – **can you die from sniffing solvents – my mate says it's the most dangerous drug you can do – is that true?** 15 year old girl.

Dear 'Can you die from sniffing solvents' – Your mate is certainly clued up. Solvents are as dangerous drugs as you can get as far as suddenly dying is concerned – and it may occur even at the first sniff. Death may be so sudden that there is no way you can get the person to a hospital.

Dear Doctor Ann – **will I get arrested if the police find me with some solvents but I'm not actually sniffing 'em?** 14 year old boy.

Dear 'Will I get arrested' – Some adolescents who have been sniffing solvents in public get picked up by the police for a variety of offences, like 'unruly behaviour in public' and 'alarming and intoxicating behaviour' or 'being in breach of the peace'. Possession of the solvent just by itself would not get you arrested. What is an offence is for a shopkeeper to supply someone under the age of 18 with a substance 'if he knows or has reasonable cause to believe that the substance or its fumes are likely to be inhaled for the purpose of causing intoxication'. It is also an offence for a shopkeeper to 'supply

any cigarette-lighter refill canister containing butane, or a substance with butane as a constituent part, to any person under the age of eighteen years'.

Dear dr ann – **recently i found my younger sister of 13 sniffing aerosols in her room bout 11:30pm.** i managed to tell my parents and it is slowly getting better but sometimes i just want to hide away and cry. people have bn supportive and everyone tells me that i just need to wait until my sister wants help but i cant because it might not happen for a couple of years depending on if she stops now or later. please could you give any suggestions on what i could actually do rather than just sitting and waiting. i really don't want to do that. Thank you. 16 year old girl.

> **Dear 'Girl with a sniffing sister'** – This must be very hard for you as there are real dangers in what she is doing. The good thing is that your parents know and she is slowly getting better. I am sure it is important that you trust her to stop the sniffing and keep on being her friend whatever happens. Sitting and waiting won't help her or you. Try doing some nice things with her so she feels valued by her big sister and has other better things to do than sitting and sniffing.

Doc – **Can glue do your head and body in?** 14 year old boy.

> **Dear 'Can glue do your head in'** – When someone is actually sniffing, they say they see strange things like hallucinations. They also occasionally lose consciousness, but normally come round without any problems. However, if they vomit whilst

they are unconscious, then there is a risk of them choking on their sick and possibly dying. When the 'sniffer' is in a dangerous place, like near a river bank or train line, accidents sometimes do happen. Very long-term, heavy use of solvents can do your head and brain in, as well as your kidneys and liver.

> *Just because these drugs are legal, it does not mean they are not dangerous. They are dangerous if used in ways that they were not designed for.*

POPPING WITH POPPERS

Doctor – **all my mates have started taking poppers.** wot r they? cos im really worried – how can i stop them and wot do they do? they came in jars n other than that i dont hav a clue but all my mates were very protective of them. plz help cos i am worried sick that i am hanging out wiv druggies. 14 year old girl.

Dear 'Mate of those doing poppers' – You're right – you are hanging out with druggies. Stay away. Poppers are also known as Liquid Gold, TNT, Amyl and Rush, amongst lots of other names. The stuff comes as a liquid in little glass bottles, which are then emptied into a hanky, or something like that, and sniffed. 'Poppers' is the common name for various chemical substances called alkyl nitrites, which include isobutyl nitrite, butyl nitrite and amyl nitrite. Nitrites are used medically to help people who are getting heart pain (called angina) to dilate the blood vessels and so get more blood to the heart muscles. Used as a 'drug', nitrites are especially popular with clubbers because it gives them a 'dance rush' by dilating the blood vessels of the brain. The effects come on immediately after inhaling it and normally last a few minutes. They are good drugs for people who need them medically, but dangerous as a fun thing.

Doc — **what are the side affects of poppers?** Age: 14. Sex: male.

Dear 'Wanting to know the side effects of poppers' – They contain chemical compounds called nitrites and are normally sniffed/inhaled. They cause blotching and reddening if they come into contact with your skin. People who inhale them a lot tend to get red sore noses. Occasionally, someone swallows the stuff instead of inhaling it and then they get a very, very sore mouth which needs urgent treatment. Side effects of inhaling poppers include headaches, flushing, dizziness and a stuffy nose. Extensive use can cause damage to the lining of the nose and to the lining of the lungs and also make you more likely to get infections. They can also be especially bad for you if you have heart trouble, asthma or eye problems. Another very real danger is that the stuff is highly flammable, so if someone is smoking at the same time as sniffing the stuff they could literally 'go up in flames'.

Dear doctor ann — **I was recently out wiv all my m8z and some of them had bought some drugs or something from this man. He said** it would get them high and it cost £5. Apparently it was a clear substance in a little bottle called poppers or something like that my friends went really hyper! R they **dangerous?** 15 year old girl.

Dear 'Person with popper-taking friends' – Poppers are dangerous. The clear fluid in the little bottle is called a nitrite and is normally taken by people with heart problems. When a person sniffs it they can feel sick, get a red face and neck and feel very light-headed, as well as getting a pounding headache. Occasionally, users can pass out, especially if they are doing some vigorous exercise like dancing at the same time. It affects the heart and should never be used with other drugs which may also be heart stimulants, like speed or ecstasy. Best thing is to tell your friends about all this – try and persuade them to stop doing them.

Dear Dr Ann – **are poppers illegal?** 17 year old boy.

Dear 'Are poppers illegal' – Nitrites are legally manufactured for medical use and being in possession of them is not illegal. People selling poppers haven't been 'had up' by the police because some nitrites have also been sold as 'room deodorizers'. However, new laws from Europe may now mean that any substance on sale which affects how we see the world or even changes a person's mood could now be classed as a medicine (whatever it is sold as) and so would come under the 'Medicines Act', which would make it illegal for anyone without a licence to prescribe or sell it.

The Speed Trap –
when everything is over the limit

Amphetamines used to be used medically to treat depression and some forms of sleep problems. There was then a craze for using them as slimming tablets, and in the 1980s they appeared on the night club scene when punk rock and Northern Soul were in fashion. Their use is very much on the down at the moment.

Dear Doc – **what is speed? One of my friends says I should try it but I'm a bit scared.** 14 year old boy.

Dear 'Scared of speed' – Speed is otherwise known as amphetamine and makes people feel confident, energetic and alert. It is usually bought as a white or pink powder. Speed, like other street drugs, has a large number of different names, like billy whiz, wake-ups, dexys, sulphate, uppers, ice. Technical names include Dexamphetamine, Dexedrine and Methamphetamine. You are right to be

85

scared to try it. It is illegal, it is addictive, and it leaves you feeling depressed and exhausted.

Dear Doc Ann — **what happens to you if you take speed?** 15 year old girl.

Dear 'Wanting to know about speed' – It increases your rate of breathing, increases the rate at which your heart beats, and decreases your appetite. This last effect made it very popular as a 'slimming' drug at one time. What most drug users take it for, however, is to keep them awake. They also take it because it makes them feel more energetic and confident, more alert and less tired. With bigger amounts, people get the impression that their physical and mental powers are improved. All these effects are temporary and there is a big 'come down' when the drug wears off.

Dear Doctor Ann — **how do people use speed and how long do the effects last?** 17 year old boy.

Dear 'Curious about speed' – Most people take speed by mouth as a white powder dissolved in a drink. But some people sniff it up their noses or occasionally inject it. Injecting the drug is definitely mad because of the dangers of getting AIDs and hepatitis and all sorts of other nasty infections. But injecting it is also totally crazy because the amount of the actual drug in the white powder that is called 'amphetamine' when bought on the street, is likely to be more than three-quarters something entirely different like de-worming powder. If speed is taken by mouth, the effects can take up to an hour to begin and can last for up to six to eight hours.

Dear Doc Ann – **i have a friend who i am so worried about. He's 14 yrs old and is a speed addict and is threatening to take an overdose because he is too depressed about his circumstances in life.** He has become paranoid and feels people are against him. It is seriously worrying me as i know he would go through with it. I don't know what to say or how to react to his comments, and i feel that if he does do it, it would be my fault for not knowing what to say. Boy aged 14.

> *Dear 'Friend of a speed addict'* –
> Whatever happens, it will not be your fault.
> It also sounds as though he really needs
> professional help which you can't give. Even
> if he says you mustn't tell anyone, this is
> one of the occasions when you must tell
> another responsible adult whom you trust,
> such as a teacher, parent or the school nurse.

Dear Doctor Ann – **What are the side effects of taking speed?** 17 year old girl.

> *Dear 'Side effects of speed'* – As they say: 'What goes up must come down'. If speed makes your body and mind work faster and depresses your appetite, then when these effects wear off, the side effects kick in and the user feels tired, depressed and very hungry. They may also feel panicky and anxious. One problem is that students sometimes use speed to

keep themselves awake to work, but amphetamines affect your ability to concentrate, and the 'come down' may arrive just when you don't need it – for example when you are taking exams.

A law came in in 1956 making it illegal to sell drugs with amphetamines in them over the counter in chemists. Up to that time, many people had used the drug legally because they were bored or felt tired all the time. It was also used by people who worked long hours, like long-distance lorry drivers. At one time in the 1960s, there was a craze of taking 'purple hearts', which was a mixture of amphetamines and barbiturates.

Dear Ann – **what happens when you take too much speed for a long time?** 16 year old boy.

Dear 'Effects of long-term speed use' – Long-term use can lead to psychological dependence on the drug and also the need to take bigger and bigger doses to have the same effect. If you do without sleep and food for long periods of time, this makes your resistance to infections lower and you may get lots of colds and other bug infections. Women who use the drug over a long period of time may get eating disorders like anorexia nervosa. Long-term users also begin to get extremes of feeling both very high and very low, and feelings of aggression along with attacks of feeling that everyone is getting at them. Occasionally they will get hallucinations.

14 Designer
dance and
chance
drug

Ecstasy is entirely artificially created. It was first made in 1914, but was not really used for anything much except some experiments by the US Army in the 1950s. It was 'rediscovered' in the 1960s and began to be made illegally. It is thought to be used by around half a million young people in the UK as a dance drug at weekends, but its use is beginning to fall off. Deaths due to ecstasy have been very high profile, but just as worrying is recent information that it might be doing your brain in.

● **WHAT IT IS LIKE AND WHAT EFFECT IT HAS**

Dear Dr ann – **what is ecstasy?** 14 year old girl.

Dear 'Wanting to know about ecstasy' – It is a drug that is an entirely artificial substance. Its chemical name is

3,4 methylenedioxymethamphetamine, or MDMA for short. It comes in the form of tablets or capsules that are taken by mouth. However, what gets sold as ecstasy may be anything but ecstasy. Sometimes there is no ecstasy in it at all and sometimes there is lots – the problem is that you never know! Ecstasy itself releases chemical messengers in the brain called 5HT. This stuff normally helps control your mood – how hungry, aggressive, sexy, etc. you feel. Ecstasy made its reputation as a 'dance' drug at the huge rave parties that took place in the 1990s. Ecstasy, like most other illegal drugs, has lots of different names, like Es, Doves, essence, love doves, M and Ms, MDMA, etc.

Dear Doc – **how does ecstasy affect the body?** 17 year old boy.

Dear 'Curious about how ecstasy affects your body' – As far as your body is concerned, ecstasy may make you feel hot and sweaty, it dries your mouth out, makes your heart beat faster, makes your pupils bigger and it may give you the shits. But then people don't take it for its effect on their bodies, but for its effect on their minds – and even that is not all good!

Doctor Ann – **my girlfriend says she has tried an E but when I ask her what its like she just says 'fun' and that doesn't help me. Can you help?** 15 year old boy.

Dear 'Boy with girlfriend trying ecstasy' – Ecstasy can affect your mind.

It is a stimulant that can also give you mild hallucinations. The effects start between half an hour and an hour after taking the drug and can last several hours. The drug seems to make people feel both calm and energetic, which is why it is used extensively as a 'dance drug'. The other effect that seems to have made it very popular at the huge rave parties is that it makes people feel increasingly 'in tune' with those around them, and any sense of anger or aggression is lost. Sounds to me as if your girlfriend has 'tuned out' if she can't tell you what it feels like herself!

Hi Doc – **What does ecstasy look like?** 16 year old boy.

Dear 'Wanting to know what ecstasy looks like' – Well, in its pure form: a white powder like an awful lot of chemical substances. But, when it is sold illegally, it has usually been transformed, so it is unlikely that you are ever going to get anything that is anywhere near a pure form. 'On the street' it is normally sold in tablet or capsule form, which can be many different colours and with many different designs on it. This may contain absolutely no ecstasy at all, a little ecstasy mixed with anything from chalk or worm medicine to speed, or it may be fairly pure. If you want to think about what ecstasy might look like – as near as you can get is if you think of an aspirin tablet and then think of all the colours of the rainbow.

Dear Doctor Ann – **what are the side effects of taking Es?** 17 year old girl.

Dear 'Ecstasy side effects' – The most obvious and worrying side effect of the drug is that since it started being used by large numbers of people in the UK, over 100 people have died as a result of taking it. And what is of very serious and increasing concern is the research evidence that use of ecstasy may lead to brain damage, with sustained loss of memory and a very real increased risk of depression. At first, ecstasy seems to increase your happiness, but after a day or two, or even up to three weeks, someone who uses the drug becomes depressed. What is most serious is that this depression seems to last, even after people have stopped using the drug.

DANGER   DANGER   DANGER   DANGER   DANGER

'ECSTASY CAN RESULT IN CRIPPLING DEPRESSION AFTER JUST A COUPLE OF OF TABLETS, A STUDY REVEALED TODAY' Observer 16th March 2003. In a study of 221 young professionals comparing ecstasy users with those who had not used it and those who took cannabis, they found that even if you use ecstasy less than 20 times, you are significantly more likely to get depressed. With those who had taken more ecstasy, the depression is even more severe. It seems very possible that a huge number of younger people are going to be on long-term antidepressants as a result of using the drug.

Dear Dr — **if I take ecstasy will I die?** 15 year old boy.

Dear 'Dying from ecstasy' – Over the last 15 years, there have been over 100 deaths in the UK from taking the drug, though it is not always clear exactly how the drug caused the death. The deaths seem to be due to:

- 'Heat stroke' – Because the drug makes you pretty hyperactive and is often taken in very hot, overcrowded places like clubs, people's temperatures may rise, their heart rate goes up, they sweat huge amounts and they don't take in enough fluid, which means that their blood tends to thicken up. Couple this with the fact that the drug also seems to make people's blood clot more than normal, then the result is that people's blood clots inside their bodies and they die.

- 'Too much fluid' – In order to stop this happening, people drink lots and lots of fluid, but ecstasy also prevents people's kidneys from working normally so that their blood gets very diluted out and they can die as a result.

- 'Heart problems' – Ecstasy causes people's blood pressure to increase and some young people who already have a heart problem collapse and die.

DO'S, DON'TS AND THE LAW

Doc — **can you tell me what to do and what not to do when you take an 'E'.** 15 year old girl.

Dear 'What to do and not to do' – Well, if you are going to try it and you are not to be put off, try to make sure that you do the following:

93

- take only small amounts at first – like a quarter of a tablet
- tell a friend what you are doing
- make sure that you are well and fit before you try it
- have enough fluid around, especially if you are dancing
- rest frequently
- ensure you can get home safely without driving
- don't take other drugs at the same time
- don't repeatedly take ecstasy without leaving a decent time interval, like a week, between. This is because ecstasy users may feel tired and have a 'come down' and need a long period of sleep between doses

Dear Doctor Ann – **my sister says she does ecstasy at weekends but I'm dead worried about her getting caught with some. What's with the law on it?** 14 year old girl.

Dear 'Worried about your sister' – Ecstasy is a class A drug, which means your sister could get up to seven years in prison and a fine for possessing it, and if she is supplying it to others, she could get a life imprisonment and a fine. If the person you supply it to dies taking it, then you may face a murder or manslaughter charge. Definitely worth worrying about, I'd say.

Tripping way
beyond reality

HALLUCINATING ON ACID AND MAGIC MUSHROOMS

There are certain drugs that give people very strong hallucinations. A hallucination is an image or sense of something real that is only happening in the mind but not actually happening in the outside world. So a hallucination has been likened to a very real dream where you may think you are flying, seeing the world from a distance, or wandering around inside someone else's head!

● TRIPPING ON LSD (LYSERGIC ACID)

Dear Doctor Ann – **can LSD (Acid) make you go insane, cause you to have panic attacks, or kill you?** 17 year old girl.

Dear 'Wondering about LSD' – Yes, it can do all these things, but the main thing is that it can give you very powerful hallucinations. These are moments where you think that what is going on in your head is actually real, but in fact is *just* in your head. These hallucinations are more likely to be unpleasant or frightening if the person using the drug is already depressed or anxious. Someone using LSD may become paranoid (thinking everyone is against them) or very anxious and panicky, especially if they are taking the drug in strange, confused surroundings like at a party. Once LSD has been taken there is no going back. It takes about 12 hours for the effects to wear off. If someone who has taken the drug becomes very anxious, reassurance by people around them can usually calm them down. Occasionally, someone taking LSD (having a 'trip') has died due to having an accident while under the drug's influence (stepping off a roof for instance, when thinking they could fly). The other problem with acid is

that some people who use the drug do later get what is known as 'flashbacks', when they 'relive' what happened during the LSD trip. So it can make you go insane, which can be disturbing for all concerned!

Doctor Ann — **what does LSD look like?** 15 year old boy.

Dear 'Curious about LSD's appearance' – LSD (lysergic acid) is, in its pure form, a white powder. However, when it is used as a street drug it is normally sold as a liquid that has been dropped onto a sheet of absorbent paper. The paper, which is like blotting paper, is then cut into little squares about the size of a stamp. These are then put in the mouth and sucked. Sometimes the liquid LSD is dropped onto a sugar lump, which is then eaten.

Dear Ann – **what are the effects of lsd?**
15 year old boy.

Dear *'What are the effects of LSD'* – Well,
above all else, the effects are that the person
taking the drug has very, very vivid hallucinations.
Both what the person sees and hears in the world
around them becomes distorted, and colours appear to be very
bright. Whether these hallucinations are pleasant or
unpleasant, in part, depends on how the person is feeling at
the time when they take the drug. These hallucinations begin
about half an hour after taking LSD and may last up to 20
hours. Some drug users say that they become ultra aware of
themselves and everything around them, others describe an
'out-of-body' feeling. Some users also say that no two 'trips'
using LSD feel the same. Occasionally, trips go badly wrong
and people say that their whole perspective and outlook on
life was changed.

Albert Hoffman was a chemist who discovered LSD in 1943. He
tried it himself and subsequently wrote 'Last Friday, April 16, 1943,
I was forced to interrupt my work in the laboratory in the middle of
the afternoon and proceed home, being affected by a remarkable
restlessness, combined with a slight dizziness. At home, I lay down
and sank into a not unpleasant intoxicated-like condition,
characterized by an extremely stimulated condition. In a dreamlike
state, with eyes closed, I perceived an uninterrupted stream of
fantastic pictures, extraordinary shapes with intense, kaleidoscopic
play of colours. After some two hours this condition faded away'.
(Albert Hofmann LSD: My problem child, *McGraw Hill 1980*)

Dear Doc – **what r magic mushrooms?** – 14 year old boy.

Dear 'What are magic mushrooms' – They are definitely not 'magic', but they are mushrooms and are also known by a whole lot of other names, like mushies, magics, liberty cap, liberties, shrooms and fly agaric. The main type used by people to have a drug effect is the liberty cap (*Psilocybe semilanceata*) but fly agaric (*Amanita muscaria*) is also sometimes used. The effects of liberty caps are similar to a mild dose of LSD and can vary greatly, depending on the mood and situation of the person eating them. People get very confused with the two different kinds of magic mushrooms because one type is much stronger than the other type – 20 to 30 liberty cap mushrooms have the same effect as one, or even part of a fly agaric mushroom.

Dear Ann – **Where do magic mushrooms grow in Worthing?** 14 year old girl.

Dear 'Looking for magic mushrooms in Worthing' – I don't know Worthing well enough to even begin to wonder about where they grow there, nor personally would I be looking for them. They tend to grow in autumn, in thick grass near the bottom of trees or bushes... but the extremely poisonous 'death cap' mushroom, which can grow in the same locations, is sometimes eaten by mistake instead of 'magic' mushrooms. These death cap mushrooms can make you very ill indeed or even kill you. The first signs of eating poisonous mushrooms (whether in Worthing or anywhere else) are stomach cramps, vomiting, diarrhoea and becoming unconscious – and needs immediate emergency treatment.

Dear Doctor Ann – **what do magic mushrooms do to you?** (what do they make you feel like.) 15 year old girl.

Dear 'Magic mushrooms wonderer' – They contain a powerful chemical called psilocybin. It is a very hallucinogenic drug, meaning that it gives you very strong hallucinations. Familiar objects are seen as unfamiliar and strange, and 'trips' on the drug may be either pleasurable or very disturbing. Other side effects include feeling sick, actually being sick, getting stiff joints and becoming uncoordinated in your movements. Strong doses may result in you becoming very disorientated.

Dear Doc – **if I take them magic mushroom things do I have effects from them straight away?** 16 year old girl.

Dear 'Instant effects from magic mushrooms' – The effects of psilocybin, which is the active bit that affects you in 'magic mushrooms', are felt about 20 minutes after eating magic mushrooms and can last from around 8 to 12 hours.

Doc – **can you show me a picture of what magic mushrooms look like 'cos how do you know you are not just taking poisonous ones or something like that?**
15 year old girl.

Dear 'What do magic mushrooms look like' – I don't think that I am in the business of providing a field guide for you as to what magic mushrooms look like. However, you will find pictures of them if you go to the site provided by Drugscope at ‹*www. drugscope.com*›. But, just remember that people do get very, very sick if they take the wrong kind of mushrooms. Best to stick to the ones that you get down the local supermarket I reckon.

Thinking of checking in your life?

HEROIN, COCAINE AND CRACK

Although the number of young people using and misusing these drugs is relatively small, they are the real, real nasties that everyone worries about, and are high-profile because of the crime associated with them. Many of the people 'hooked' on these drugs are taking them because they make them feel better than they feel facing their 'real' lives without the drug. But living on these drugs is about as unglamorous an existence as you can get – a circle of crime, violence and desperation, with the odd 'high' in between.

● UNHEROIC HEROIN

Doc – **why do people take heroin? How do they do it?** 17 year old boy.

> *Dear 'Wondering why people take heroin* – People take heroin

because it makes them feel good about themselves, and safe and warm. It is a type of escape-from-reality drug, and addicts are often people who feel that their 'real' life without the drug is intolerable because of poverty, unhappiness, or mental health problems. It comes as a brown or white powder that can be sniffed, smoked in tin foil, swallowed, or diluted in water and injected. It is a very seductive and addictive drug.

Dr – **What are the main risks of taking heroin?** 14 year old boy.

Dear 'Risk enquirer' – The dangers – 'street' heroin is mixed in with all sorts of substances so you don't know what you are getting for your money. Because many heroin users inject the drug, there are all the dangers of getting Aids and hepatitis that come with injecting anything into your blood by using dirty needles that have been used by someone who has Aids. It is very difficult to give up, and when people do try and give up, they get all sorts of nasties like muscle cramps, vomiting, sweating, anxiety and the shakes. This is all to say nothing of getting arrested by the police, put into jail and fined huge sums of money.

Heroin use in the UK has increased in recent years, with the number of people arrested in connection with heroin rising over the past five years from 6000 to 8800. Deaths from heroin are around the 300 per year mark and continue to rise. Heroin is a class A drug, which means a maximum of seven years in prison and a fine for possession, and 'life' in prison with a fine, for dealing.

Dear Doctor Ann – **what r the side effects of taking heroin?** 15 year old girl.

Dear 'Side effects of heroin' – Even the first time someone uses the drug they may feel sick, get bad headaches and may throw up. Apart from the risk of getting Aids and hepatitis, there is the nasty side effect that because heroin is expensive, people usually have to turn to crime in order to pay for the habit.

Dr – **I have started to take small amounts of heroin and i am worried about the effects they could have on me can you please help me?** 15 year old girl.

Dear 'User of small amounts of heroin' – The main problems you are going to face are:

- heroin is very addictive, so it is difficult to come off it. I suggest that while you are just taking small amounts you try and stop NOW
- you are never going to know how pure the heroin is.
- it messes with your life
- you will need to take bigger and bigger doses of heroin to have the same effect
- you don't say if you are injecting – if you are, then there are all the risks associated with this, like getting Aids, hepatitis, other infections and being poisoned
- the legal penalties for possessing and dealing in heroin are extremely heavy.

Dr ann – **what are the symptoms of a heroin overdose?** 17 year old girl.

Dear 'Wanting to know the symptoms of heroin overdose' – The most immediate symptoms are your heart beating very fast, shortness of breath and becoming unconscious. When unconscious, the person may throw up and choke on their vomit.

Doctor – **just how addictive is heroin?**
15 year old girl.

Dear 'How addictive is heroin' – It is very addictive, and getting off it is difficult because of the aches and tremors and sweating and spasms that withdrawal from the drug causes. These immediate effects usually last about a week, but it may be months before someone who has stopped taking the drug feels well again. Usually, people who are being withdrawn from the drug are given another drug called methadone, because it is taken by mouth and the dose can be carefully controlled, but it is considered to be as addictive as heroin itself.

CRACKING UP ON COCAINE

Dear Doctor Ann – **can you tell me more about cocaine?** 14 year old boy.

Dear 'Curious about cocaine' – Cocaine is a chemical that was first extracted from the leaves of the coca plant in the mid-1800s. Prior to that time, many people in South America, where the coca plant grows, had chewed the leaves because it gave them a high. When Coca Cola was first made, it included a few milligrams of cocaine, but it became obvious that cocaine was very addictive. The use of it was banned and Coca Cola replaced the cocaine with caffeine – which is still in it nowadays. Cocaine comes in several forms – most commonly as a white crystalline powder that is usually sniffed, but can be dissolved in water and injected, which is even more dangerous. The people selling cocaine often mix it with other cheaper drugs, like amphetamine, that are indistinguishable in appearance from cocaine.

Dr ann – **what effects does cocaine have on the body?** 14 year old girl.

Dear 'Wanting to know the effects of cocaine' – The drug stimulates lots of different bits of the body and mind. People start taking it because within a few minutes, they start to feel good in themselves and about life, feel more self-confident, great and powerful, have more energy, more sex drive, less appetite and feel generally happy. BUT BUT BUT, within 30 minutes this starts to wear off. There are so many possible bad effects that it's difficult to mention them all. Some of the bad things about cocaine are that it makes you anxious, agitated, sweaty, dizzy, raises your blood pressure and can cause fits. The feeling after being on cocaine (the come down) can make you depressed and tired. The long-term problems of taking cocaine are also serious as it can permanently damage nerves and blood vessels in the brain, cause hallucinations and long-term depression. If you snort cocaine, it can eat away the middle of your nose so you have one rather than two nostrils! Though it has a reputation for being a 'rich man's' drug, even rich people who are hooked on it will tell you that being addicted is not at all glamorous. As soon as you've taken the cocaine, you want more, and the more you take the *less* you feel the good effects.

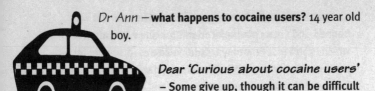

Dr Ann — **what happens to cocaine users?** 14 year old boy.

Dear 'Curious about cocaine users' – Some give up, though it can be difficult but not impossible. People who have been frequent users often start to feel tired, panicky, exhausted, unhappy and are unable to sleep when they give up and want to start taking it again to feel better. They may also get diarrhoea, vomiting, the shakes, anorexia and sweating, which for some can prove unbearable. Many chronic users are well aware of these symptoms, and in an attempt to avoid them as well as the inevitable feeling of desperate tiredness, are very reluctant to stop. If a girl gets pregnant and takes cocaine, it can damage the baby and even cause it to be addicted to cocaine when it is born. Some cocaine users get into trouble with the police and the law because they are found in possession of the drug and because they steal and rob to get the money to buy the cocaine.

● **SNAP, CRACK AND POP – YOU'RE HOOKED**

Doctor Ann — **what is the difference between crack and cocaine?** Seems like people use the words 4 the same things? 16 year old boy.

Dear 'Crack and cocaine differences' – Crack is a pure form of cocaine and is usually sniffed up the nose. It gets its name from the cracking sound it makes when it is heated as it is being prepared. It gets into the bloodstream very quickly and gives people a high for about ten minutes, followed by a real, real downer. Crack has all the same effects as cocaine, but is even more addictive and tends to give violent mood swings. Crack use is on the increase in certain inner-city areas and is particularly linked to violent crime because people addicted to crack will do almost anything to ensure they have a supply of the drug.

Cocaine is for some an expensive drug and is closely associated with the rich lifestyle enjoyed by rock and film stars. For most users, however, it is just a poor substitute for having a life. It is a class A drug, which means a maximum of seven years in prison and a fine for possession, and 'life' in prison plus a fine, for dealing. There were 2718 arrests in the UK for crack possession/dealing in 2000.

Dr – **what happens when u smoke crack?** 15 year old girl.

Dear 'What happens when you smoke crack' – The feelings of power, energy, happiness, self-confidence, and general feel-good factor – sometimes called a high – happen within a few minutes. These may last for about ten minutes and are followed by restlessness, nausea, hyperactivity, problems sleeping and the desire to have more crack. People who use crack regularly tend to get anxious, depressed, lose weight, have problems concentrating, feel exhausted and may become paranoid.

Help Dr ann – **my mate offered me crack what would u do?** 15 year old girl.

Dear 'Girl whose mate offered her crack' – Say NO. She's no mate if she is trying to get you to take crack – it's not something you want to give to your worst enemy.

A Sporting Chance
of losing everything

ALL ABOUT SPORTS DRUGS

For some, winning, whether honestly or dishonestly, seems to have become more important than the sport itself. Sports people are taking more and more drugs that enhance performance. As a result, drug testing on people taking part in sports has also become more common and more sophisticated, with the result that more people are getting 'caught' cheating.

● **THE ATHLETE AND THE DRUGS**

Dear Doctor Ann — **why do all those sport people take drugs when they know they'll get found out. Stupid I reckon?** girl age 14.

Dear 'Puzzled about sports people taking drugs' – Sport,

both professional and amateur, has become more and more competitive, and unfortunately, people have looked at ways to get one up on the others by using drugs. This, of course, is both cheating and dangerous. There are five main categories of drug that are banned by the sports authorities:

- Anabolic steroids – a group of chemicals, including nandrolone, related to testosterone which occurs naturally in the body. These help athletes build muscle and recover faster from training and injury, but they have nasty side effects
- Peptide hormones – these are chemical drugs that occur naturally in the body but can also be made artificially. They produce similar effects to the anabolic steroids.
- Strong analgesic painkillers – such as morphine and other opiates, which allow the athlete to do things that would otherwise be too painful
- Stimulants – drugs like amphetamines and cocaine, which can raise the heart rate and may improve performance
- Diuretics – chemicals that help the body to lose fluids, and are especially used by boxers to meet their fighting weight, and also to mask the presence of other banned drugs

There are other types of drugs that are only allowed under certain conditions. These include local anaesthetics, and drugs used to treat medical conditions, such as cortico-steroids (used to treat asthma) and beta-blockers (used to treat heart conditions). Even some special vitamin drinks and fitness supplements contain substances that make an athlete test positive. As drug tests are carried out in a large number of sports, it seems crazy to take the risk. In the USA, more young people taking part in sport at

school are being tested as well – something that will, without
doubt, soon come to the UK.

● HOW TO GET THAT RIPPLING MUSCLE EFFECT

Dear dr ann – **My muscles are really weedy and
I want to get into the football team but need to
build my muscles up?** Boy aged 13.

Dear 'Wanting big muscles' – It sounds
as though you haven't gone through puberty
yet, and when this does happen, you will get taller and
stronger and your muscles will also get bigger thanks to your
natural hormones. Eating a good diet, with five pieces of fruit
or vegetables a day, along with exercise, is the best way to
make the muscles you have strong and good for football.
There's no need to take anything else, and if anyone suggests
taking steroids or any other body-building things, say no. They
are dangerous, and if you take them before puberty they may
stop you getting as tall as you would have done.

Dear Dr Ann – **are there some drugs I can
take to make me stronger without anyone
knowing?** Boy age 15.

Dear 'Wanting to be stronger' – The
answer to this is NO. People do it all the
time and they get caught doing it all the
time. The best way to make your muscles stronger is to do
regular exercise – running, swimming and other sports will all
help. You may see pictures of 'strong men' lifting weights,
whose bodies look totally weird. Some of these men and

women will have taken anabolic steroids to develop their muscles, but it is against sporting rules to use almost any drugs and take part in competitive sports. Even if you just want to take them to be stronger, they are dangerous. As well as increasing muscle strength, they can damage the liver, make you very moody, increase the risk of cancer, cause acne, make men have breasts, give women hair on their face, make you bald and cause men to have difficulty getting erections. The weightlifters and discus throwers from the former East Germany who won many Olympic gold medals are now getting very ill as a result of the diet of steroid-type drugs they were given. Best stick to exercise and give these drugs a miss.

Dear dr Ann – **My friend read this article about girls taking steroids to make them fitter and have better sex – is it true and can my doctor prescribe them?** Girl aged 15.

Dear 'Curious about steroids and sex' – Your doctor will sometimes need to prescribe various different steroids to people for a medical condition. But doctors should not prescribe steroids for the reasons you are suggesting. There have been some reports from the USA of girls getting hold of types of steroids illegally to build up muscles and improve their sex life, though there is little evidence that they improve anyone's sex lives! These drugs are dangerous and also cause other unpleasant side effects, such as acne, depression and high blood pressure, even when you have to take them for a disease or medical problem, so they should never be taken for frivolous reasons.

Dear Doc — **I have asthma and am in the athletics team at school. My friend says it's not fair if I use my puffer to help before I run but otherwise I get too wheezy.**

Dear 'Asthmatic athlete' – Please do continue to use your asthma inhaler and don't give up on being in the athletics team. There is no problem in using the anti-asthma drugs for the type of sport you are involved in. Anyone who decides to take up sport professionally should discuss any drugs they need to take for a medical condition – whether for asthma, diabetes or whatever – with their trainer or person in charge.

Anabolic steroids are drugs that come under the **Medicines Act**, which means that you can only legally get them by getting a doctor's prescription for them, and they can only be sold to you by a chemist when you have a doctor's prescription. Anabolic steroids are class C drugs under the **Misuse of Drugs Act**. But, like tranquillisers, just possessing them is not something that the police can arrest you for. Therefore you can't get arrested just because you have anabolic steroids for your own use, even without a prescription from a doctor. It is, however, an offence to supply them to someone else.

Getting tested
getting busted

Almost 100,000 people in the UK are caught each year by the police with cannabis, and nine out of ten of those people caught are considered to be 'in possession' of the drug for personal use. The other one in ten are done for 'dealing'. In the past, of all the people caught 'in possession' of cannabis, over half received a caution rather than being arrested and taken to court. More recently, however, 'cautioning' has become even more common, especially for people being caught for the first time. Luckily, 'cautioning' does *not* mean that you get a criminal conviction. However, it does go down on police records and you are given a stern warning. If you are found guilty in court of possessing cannabis, you do get a criminal conviction. That stops you being able to hold a number of jobs, especially jobs in which you may have to look after children, but also if you want to join the police or the legal profession.

Dr ann – **tell me how long drugs can be detected in your body please, 'cos I'm worried 'cos I do drugs sometimes but don't want to get the police on me and I'm worried.** 15 year old boy.

Dear 'Worried about drug tests' – The main method used for testing people for drugs is a urine test. There is a wide range of drugs that can be tested for in this way – and drugs do continue to come out in your pee for some time after you have used a drug. If you have your urine tested for drugs, the positive detection time after taking the actual drug is as follows:

- Alcohol   12–24 hours
- Amphetamine   2–4 days
- Cannabis   2–7 days, but up to one month for regular users
- Cocaine/crack   12 hours – 3 days
- Ecstasy   2–4 days
- Heroin   1–2 days
- LSD (Lysergic acid)   2–3 days

In some circumstances, you may be asked to have a blood test, for which the detection times are still about the same as above. Using a drug way back can also be detected using people's hair, though this is a less reliable method.

Drug testing is being used more and more, both at people's work places and in sport. Nowadays, it is even spreading to some schools, particularly public schools, where they have begun to drug test their students. Home testing kits are not all that accurate, although they are becoming popular in the USA.

Dear Dr Ann – **If you were caught in possession of drugs would you get taken to jail?** if yes for how long. 13 year old girl.

> *Dear 'Would you go to jail'* – What happens if you are arrested using a drug first depends on how much you are caught in possession of. If you are thought to be 'dealing' in an illegal drug (selling it to others), then you are likely to go to prison for longer. With drugs like heroin and cocaine, if you are convicted for possession, it can lead to a maximum sentence of seven years in prison and a fine. The maximum sentence for selling it to others is 'life' imprisonment and a fine. For drugs like amphetamine (speed) or barbiturates, the maximum sentence for possession is five years and a fine. If you sell it to others, then you can get up to 14 years in prison and a fine. For cannabis and anabolic steroids, the maximum sentence is two years for possessing them and five years if you are dealing in them.

● **LEGAL SITUATION**

> *Dear Dr Ann* – **is it legal for me to smoke cannabis??** 17 year old boy.

> *Dear 'Cannabis smoker'* – No, it is still illegal for you to smoke cannabis.

Dear Doctor – **what is the new legal situation about cannabis?** Can you still get arrested if you are just using it just 4 yourself? 15 year old boy.

Dear 'Wondering about the new legal situation with cannabis' – I am not surprised that you may be confused, and it is difficult to know exactly what the situation is just at this very moment. Cannabis is presently (2003) being reclassed as a class C drug. This means that it will remain illegal but with reduced penalties. There will be a maximum sentence of two years for possession and five years for dealing. But, if you are stopped by the police and are found to have cannabis on you, you have an increased chance of getting away with just a 'warning' or a 'caution'. But remember, you could still also get taken to court!

Dear dr Ann – **Why are drugs illegal?** 14 year old boy.

Dear 'Why are drugs illegal' – What is considered to be legal or illegal in our country depends on what 'rules' or 'laws' our government decides there should be. We (adults) elect the government, so we (young people and adults) have to play by these rules whether we like them or not – or risk the consequences, prison and fines! These rules or laws are there to protect the individuals who live in that country. An obvious rule, which, if we didn't obey it without questioning, would cause us a lot of trouble, is stopping at red traffic lights. Other laws exist to stop one group of people harming another group of people. An example of this are the laws stopping grown-ups from sexually abusing children. Drugs have been made illegal because they harm people's health, they make people behave in odd ways, they are addictive, and people are bullied into using them by those trying to sell them. You could say that they also cause a lot of crime, but that is a rather strange argument because if they weren't against the law, then you wouldn't have so much drug-related crime – sort of chicken and egg situation.

Dear Dr Ann — **Will drugs become legal?** 13 year old girl.

Dear 'Wondering if drugs will become legal' – I don't think that some drugs will ever become legal. Cannabis has been so-called 'decriminalized', which means that it is still illegal but you are (a) less severely punished for using it (b) less likely to get arrested for using it. The worst illegal drugs like heroin and cocaine/crack are likely to remain illegal because of all the health problems that they cause. The people who want the legalization of drugs argue that it is the right of individual adults to decide for themselves what is good or bad for them and that they should be allowed to do things that endanger their own lives as long as they don't endanger the lives of others. The other argument for at least making drugs less of a crime is that if you absolutely forbid people to do something, it simply doesn't work. This was shown in America when they tried to outlaw all alcohol sales and use. Crime related to alcohol soared up and became impossible to control.

The two main laws governing drug use in the UK

The Medicines Act 1968 *is to do with the manufacture and supply of medicines and rarely affects the general public. It divides drugs into three categories. The most restricted drugs can only be obtained on prescription.*

The Misuse of Drugs Act 1971 *is intended to prevent the non-medical use of certain drugs. It covers not only medicines but also drugs with no medical uses. There are a series of different offences under this act, including unlawful supply, intent to supply, import or export (all these are collectively known as 'trafficking' offences), and unlawful production. To enforce this law the police have powers to stop, detain and search people on 'reasonable suspicion' that they are in possession of an illegal drug.*

Damage limitation –
knowing the facts

The best way to avoid trouble with illegal drugs is to avoid taking them, and certainly to avoid dealing in them. But if you do try them, it is a very good idea to do it as safely as possible and to know what to do if things go wrong. Similarly, if you or friends start to have a drug problem, you will need to know where to get help.

● **TAKING PRECAUTIONS**

Dear Doc – **I'm planning to go to a club next month with a friend and his older brother and we are planning to drop some pills. Don't tell me not to cos our minds are made up but what precautions can we take before and during the night?** 15 year old boy.

Dear 'Pill dropper' – OK, here are some basic rules if you are going to take drugs:

- Make sure that you do it with friends so that they can help you (and you, them) if you get into trouble and/or when you 'come down' after the drugs
- Know a bit of first aid – in case your friends get into trouble

- Try not to get your drugs from strangers – you never know what will be in them
- Remember that the way drugs make you feel will, to some extent, depend on how you are feeling before you take them – so don't take them if you are feeling depressed or anxious
- Always make sure that you know what you are taking and what your friends are taking, so if you get into trouble you know what each of you has had
- If you were over 17, I would tell you not to drive
- Remember, there is a high risk of you getting ripped off for what you pay for your drugs because drug dealers are unscrupulous
- Remember, if you are caught with illegal drugs by the police, you may get prosecuted, fined, sent to prison (depending on your age) and get a criminal record, which may affect your ability to get a job in the future
- Be especially careful if you are already taking some drug prescribed by your own doctor
- With some 'clubbing' drugs like ecstasy, make sure you have access to water and that the club is not too hot or overcrowded
- Read this book before you do anything else!

Dear Doctor Ann – **my mate is doing drugs. What can I do to stop him?** Boy age 16.

Dear 'Person with a mate doing drugs' – Around half of all teenagers will experiment with taking illegal drugs, and half will stay well away from them. With those 'experimenting' with drugs, this will mostly be smoking a bit of cannabis. What

you really need to worry about with your mate is whether he is actually 'hooked' on drugs (sort of addicted). Best thing is to talk to him about it and try and find out why he is doing them. You may not be able to get him to stop, but it will certainly help him to have someone he can talk to about it.

Dear Dr Ann – **Please please please answer this cos I am soooo worried about my best friend! I hang around with a pretty rough crowd – not on purpose – they just kinda turn up but any ways.**

Pretty much all of them smoke hash and just normal fags. Yesterday my best friend H**** came down off the field looking pretty woozy and she had to go home from school. She was away today and when I try to ring her mum just says that she is ill. I don't want to lose my best friend what can I do? 15 year old girl.

Dear 'Worried about best friend' – Great that you want to help, but don't think that you can do this alone. Try talking to your friend about it and see if you can persuade her that she needs help. Wanting help with drug use is the huge first step. Next – where to get help. Give her the phone number of the drugs telephone helpline (0800 776600) and suggest she looks at the BBC site on drugs or *www.drugscope.org.uk*, which gives good information on drugs and where to get help. You might try talking to your parents first about what to do, as you do not have to keep this information to yourself. Most important of all, don't feel you have to be the same as this group of friends for them to still like you – stick with your views that drugs and smoking aren't for you. Good luck.

Dear Dr Ann – **Can you stop drugs?** 13 year old boy.

Dear 'Can you stop drugs' – Yes, yes, yes. It is easier to give up some drugs than others. But even for the most difficult ones such as crack and cocaine, most people who want to give up manage to, though they may need help from special drug treatment clinics, doctors, friends and counsellors.

Dear Dr Ann – **Hey I think I need help about drugs and smoking. How can I stop b4 I cause some serious damage.** 17 year old boy.

Dear 'Needing help to give up drugs' – You have taken the most important step in deciding you want to give up. Make a list of the drugs you are doing, including tobacco. Write down when you do these drugs, when you smoke, and who with, so that you really understand the extent of the problem. Don't try to tackle everything at once. You should probably try giving up the illegal drugs first and concentrate on not smoking tobacco later. Try to avoid the situations and friends when and with whom you know you will be tempted to take the drugs. Reward yourself by spending the money you would have used on drugs to do other nice things. Go and talk to your doctor about what help is available locally – all you say will be treated confidentially.

Dear Ann – **should you tell your parents if you take drugs?** 13 year old girl.

Dear 'Should you tell your parents' – By far the best thing is to have discussed illegal drugs in general with your parents *before* you even think of taking them yourself. It would be good for you to know what your parents' attitude is towards them and how they would react if you were taking them. It would also give your parents a chance to think how they might react if they get a sudden call to the local cop shop in the middle of the night to bail you out! Remember, parents are very good at guessing when their children are taking drugs or doing anything else they aren't meant to be doing, as they were young once themselves.

QUIZ 3 THE REAL NASTIES...

1 The maximum prison sentence for:
- ☐ a dealing in cannabis is going to be 5 years
- ☐ b selling heroin is 10 years
- ☐ c possessing ecstasy is 7 years

2 The following are true about ecstasy:
- ☐ a it can affect your memory
- ☐ b it makes you violent
- ☐ c it is normally pure when you get it

3 It is true that:
- ☐ a crack is a pure form of cocaine
- ☐ b crack is less addictive than cocaine
- ☐ c you can never get off cocaine because it is so addictive

4 Sniffing solvents (glue, lighter fluid, paint thinner, etc.)
- ☐ a gets commoner as people get older
- ☐ b can cause you to suddenly drop dead
- ☐ c is safer than most other drugs

5 Which of the following give you hallucinations?
- ☐ a cannabis
- ☐ b magic mushrooms
- ☐ c heroin

If you got them all right, you are really clued up.
If you got them all wrong – read this book again, because you are kidding yourself that you know anything about the drug scene, and probably think that drugs are much less harmful than they are.

Answers

1: **a and c are correct.** Selling heroin or even ecstasy could get you 'life'.

2: **a is correct.** Most ecstasy is 'cut' (mixed) with everything under the sun. It is a class A drug and people have died from using it.

3: **a is correct.** Crack is even more addictive than cocaine, but remember that help is always available, whatever you are addicted to.

4: **b is the correct one.** Sniffing solvents is definitely dangerous from the point of view of suddenly dropping down dead!

5: **a, b and c are all correct** but cannabis doesn't usually give hallucinations unless you are using one of the stronger forms.

Need to find out more?

Websites for teenagers

www.teenagehealthfreak.org
www.doctorann.org
Two linked websites for young people. Read the daily diary of Pete Payne aged 15 – all about his problems with his zits, sex life and sister. Leap to Doctor Ann's virtual surgery for all you want to know about fatness and farting, sex and stress, drinking and drugs, pimples and periods, hormones and headaches, and a million other things.

http://news.bbc.co.uk/1/hi/health/1615851.stm
A website which provides you with lots of detailed information about a wide range of different drugs both legal and illegal.

www.drugscope.org.uk/druginf
Lots of detailed information about individual drugs and where to get help.

All your problems
ChildLine
Royal Mail Building, Studd Street London NW1 0QW
Freepost 1111, London N1 0BR
Tel: 020 7239 1000
Helpline: 0800 1111 (24 hours a day, every day of the year)
www.childline.org.uk

Provides a national telephone helpline for children and young people in danger or distress, who want to talk to a trained counsellor. All calls are free and confidential.

Alcohol
Drinkline
National Alcohol Helpline – 0800 917 8282 (9 am–11 pm, Mon–Fri, 6 pm–11 pm Sat–Sun)
Advice and information about alcohol.

National Association for Children of Alcoholics
Helpline: 0800 358 3456
Help and information for young people whose parents have a drink problem.

Bullying
Anti-Bullying Campaign
185 Tower Bridge Road, London SE1 2UF Tel: 020 7378 1446
Gives telephone advice for young people who are being bullied.

Bullying Helpline
Tel: 0850 449944
Gives advice to children who are being bullied.

Kidscape
Tel: 020 7730 3300
Information for children on keeping safe from bullying.

Cigarettes and smoking

QUIT

Quitline: 0800 002200
www.quit.org.uk
Want to give up smoking? Phone this line for help. Open 1 pm–9 pm.

Down, depressed, anxious or suicidal

The Samaritans

Helpline: 08457 909090
www.samaritans.org.uk
Someone will always listen to you and your problems any time of the day or night and it costs nothing for the call.

Drugs

National Drugs Helpline

Tel: 0800 776600
www.ndh.org.uk
A free 24-hour, 365-days-a-year confidential service available in English and other languages. The helpline gives information, advice and counselling, offering constructive and supportive referrals and literature to callers with concerns about drugs and solvents. Gives information about local services.

CRIMESTOPPER SNAP
Say No And Phone CAMPAIGN

Tel: 0800 555111 (free call)
SNAP is the nationwide Crime stoppers campaign aimed at tackling the drug problem. You can call anonymously (you won't be asked your name, address or phone number) if you know anyone who regularly supplies drugs or who commits any crime.

Release

388 Old Street, London EC1V 9LT
Advice Line: 020 7729 9904
(10 am–5 pm, Mon–Fri)
24-hour Emergency Line:
020 7603 8654
Drugs in Schools: 0345 366666
(10 am–5 pm, Mon–Fri)
Heroin help line: 020 7749 4053
www.release.org.uk
Confidential service for drug-related legal problems. Concerned with the welfare of users (of both illegal and prescribed drugs) and their family and friends. Offers emergency help in cases of arrest.

Families Anonymous

Tel: 020 7498 4680
For families and friends of drug users – self-help group.

Parents Against Drug Abuse

24-hour service: 08457 023867
Offers help and information for parents and families of drug users.

Resolve

Tel: 080 8800 2345 (free line, Mon–Fri 9.00–5.00)

Help with all drug problems

If you are ill

NHS Direct Tel: 0845 4647
www.nhsdirect.nhs.uk
Information and help about drugs
or any problems caused by drugs.
Talk to a nurse on the phone about
any health problem.

HIV/Aids

National Aids Helpline

Tel: 0800 567123 (free and
confidential) available 24 hours a
day, 7 days a week
Questions or worries about Aids
can be discussed with a trained
adviser.

Sex and everything attached

Brook Advisory Service

Young people's helpline:
0800 0185 023
User-friendly information service –
will tell you all about local clinics
and send you leaflets even if you
are under 16.

fpa (formerly the Family Planning Association)

2–12 Pentonville Road,
London N1 9FP
Tel: 020 7837 5432
Helpline: 020 7837 4044
(9 am–7 pm, Mon–Fri)
Gives information on all aspects of
contraception and sexual health.
Free fun leaflets available. They
also run a telephone helpline for

anyone who wants information on
contraception and sexual health.
Phone the helpline number to find
the nearest fpa clinic in your area.

Rape Crisis Helplines

Look in the telephone directory or
ring Directory Enquiries on 192 for
the Helpline number in your area.
Provide free confidential support
and advice to victims of rape.

Lesbian and Gay Switchboard

Tel: 020 7837 7324 (24 hours a day)
www.llgs.org.uk
(this is the London and national
Switchboard; there are also a
number of regional switchboards)
Offers information and advice to
lesbians and gay men and their
families and friends.

Sexwise

Tel: 0800 282 930
Gives information to young people
up to 21 about sex.

General help

Get connected

Tel: 0808 808 4994
For young people, offers external
support, especially those running
away from home or who have left
home already.

Teenage home

Tel: 0800 700 740 (24-hour line)
For children who have already run
away and want to get in touch but
are scared.

Index

A

acne 111
addiction 11, 12, 16, 20–21,
    22–23, 70–71, 101, 120
Aids 34, 86, 102, 103
alcohol 15, 27, 49–57, 114
    calories in 55
    death resulting from
        use 35, 57
    drinking during
        pregnancy 33, 54
    effects 34, 53–57
    mixing with cannabis
        70
    units of 50–51, 52
allergic reactions 9
amphetamines 10, 15, 16,
    35, 84, 85–88, 105, 109,
    114, 115
amyl see poppers
anabolic steroids 16,
    109–112, 115
anorexia nervosa 88, 106
antibiotics 9, 33, 55–56
antidepressants 55, 75, 92
anxiety 12, 73, 87, 96, 119

B

babies 32–35, 54, 74–75,
    106
barbiturates 11, 16, 115
beer 49, 51, 52, 55; see
    also alcohol
benzodiazepines 12
binge drinking 51
blood clots 93
blood pressure 46, 59, 69,
    93, 111
brain damage 13, 33, 46,
    89, 92, 105
breath, bad 43, 44, 45
bronchitis 77
bulimia 54–55
bullying 20, 24–29, 47,
    116

C

caffeine 9, 36–39
California orange see skunk
cancer 45, 46, 56, 60, 68,
    77, 111

cannabis 14, 15, 16, 17, 29,
    58–64, 113, 114, 115–117
    cost 75
    dependency on 22, 61,
        70–71, 77
    and depression 21
    eating 59, 63–64, 66
    effects 31, 58–61, 63,
        65–77
    forms of 31
    mixing with alcohol 70
    resin 31, 62
    smoking 22, 59, 61,
        63–64, 66, 67,
        69–70, 74–77, 115,
        121
chocolate 37, 39
cider 49, 52; see also
    alcohol
cigarettes see tobacco
class A drugs 15–16, 102
class B drugs 15–16
class C drugs 15–16, 116
cocaine 10, 15, 16, 101,
    104–106, 109, 114, 115,
    117, 121
    addiction to 22, 29,
        101, 105, 106
    crack see crack cocaine
    injecting 105
    use during pregnancy
        33
cocoa 36–39
coffee 9, 36–39
cola 36–39
contraceptive pill 46
crack cocaine 16, 17, 22,
    101, 106–107, 114, 121
crime 103, 107, 116, 119

D

dance drugs 83, 90–91, 119
dealing 113, 115, 116
death following drug use
    32, 35, 79–80, 96
    alcohol 35, 57
    ecstasy 35,
    magic mushrooms 99
    tobacco 16, 35, 41,
        46–47, 69
dependency on drugs 11,
    22, 70–71, 77, 88; see
    also addiction
depression 21–22, 27, 119

alcohol 54, 55
amphetamines 86–87
anabolic steroids 111
cannabis 60–61, 68, 71,
    73–74
cocaine 105
ecstasy 92
LSD 96
dexys see amphetamines
diuretics 109
dope see cannabis
drinking see alcohol
driving 52, 53, 70, 119
drunk, getting 50–51, 53

E

ecstasy 10, 15, 16, 31, 84,
    89–94, 114, 119
    death resulting from
        use 35, 89, 92–94
emphysema 46
endorphins 10
ethanol 49
exercise 10

F

financial costs 28, 32,
    75–76, 103
fines 115, 119
flashbacks 96
fly agaric see magic
    mushrooms

G

ganga see cannabis
glue sniffing see solvents
grass 31; see also cannabis

H

hallucinations 81, 88, 91,
    95–100, 105
hangovers 56
hash 31; see also cannabis
hash brownies 66
heart disease 45, 46, 77
hepatitis 34, 86, 102, 103
heroin 10, 11, 15, 16,
    101–104, 114, 115, 117
    addiction to 22, 29,
        101–102, 103, 104
    death resulting from
        use 35
    injecting 34–35, 102,
        103

use during pregnancy 33–35
HIV 34–35

I
illegal drugs 8, 9, 10–11, 113, 116–117
impotence 44–45, 57, 65–66, 111
infertility 66–67
injecting drugs 34–35, 86, 102, 103, 105

J
joints see cannabis

K
kidney damage 82, 93

L
lager 50; see also alcohol
legal drugs 8–9, 11
liberty cap (liberties) see magic mushrooms
Liquid Gold see poppers
liver damage 54, 56, 57, 82, 111
LSD 16, 31, 95–97, 114
lung cancer 45, 56, 68
lung disease 45, 46–47, 61, 77
lysergic acid see LSD

M
M and Ms see ecstasy
magic mushrooms 98–100
marijuana see cannabis
MDMA see ecstasy
medical drugs 8–9, 12, 17, 33, 112, 119
memory loss 61, 73, 92
mental illness 54, 60–61, 68, 71, 73–74, 96
methadone 10, 16, 104
morphine 10, 35, 109
multiple sclerosis 60

N
nabilone 67–68
needles 34–35, 86, 102
nicotine 41, 45; see also tobacco
nitrites see poppers
number of drug users 10,

13–15, 23, 44, 58, 120

O
overdose 9, 11, 103–104

P
painkillers 109
paranoia 96
passive smoking 21, 45, 48
penicillin 9
penis
  and cannabis 65–66
  and drinking 57
  and smoking 44–45
peptide hormones 109
poppers 10, 82–84
possession 113, 115, 116
pot see cannabis
pregnancy 32–35, 54, 74–75, 106
prison 115–116, 119
puff see cannabis
pushers 20, 25–26, 116, 119

Q
reasons for drug use 19–23, 24, 41–44, 58, 101–102
reefers see cannabis
relationships, drugs affecting 30–32
road accidents 52, 53
Rohypnol 28–29

S
schizophrenia 60–61, 68, 73–74
schools' drugs policy 18, 114
shit see cannabis
shrooms see magic mushrooms
side effects 16
signs of drug-taking 30–31
skunk 62
slimming drugs 16, 85, 86
smoking see cannabis; crack cocaine; tobacco
solvents 35, 79–82
speed see amphetamines
sperm production 34, 45, 67
spiked drinks 28–29

spirits 52; see also alcohol
spliffs see cannabis
sports drugs 108–112
steroids see anabolic steroids
stomach ulcers 54
sulphate see amphetamines
syringes 34–35, 86, 102

T
tea 9, 36–39
teeth and smoking 44
testing for drugs 63–64, 108, 114
THC 59
tobacco 14, 15, 41–48
  addiction to 16, 20, 22, 41, 45, 47–48, 76
  cost of smoking 28, 46
  death resulting from use 16, 35, 41, 46–47, 69
  health risks 44–45, 46, 67, 77
  passive smoking 21, 45, 48
  smoking cannabis with 22, 61, 67, 69–70, 75–77
  smoking and weight 42–43
  stopping smoking 47, 122
  use during pregnancy 33, 74
  why people smoke 20–21, 41–44
tripping 95–100

U
uppers see amphetamines

V
valium 12, 16

W
weed see cannabis
wine 49, 52; see also alcohol